I0137146

# Staff Ride Handbook for the Battle of Shiloh, 6-7 April 1862

LTC Jeffrey J. Gudmens
and the Staff Ride Team
Combat Studies Institute

Cover photo: "Pittsburg Landing After the Battle of Shiloh," #68448, Naval Historical Center, Washington Navy Yard, DC.

**Published by Books Express Publishing**
**Copyright © Books Express, 2012**
**ISBN 978-1-78039-794-8**

**Books Express publications are available from all good retail and online booksellers. For publishing proposals and direct ordering please contact us at: info@books-express.com**

# Contents

# Illustrations

## Tables

## Maps

# Foreword

Since the early 20th century the US Army has used Civil War and other battlefields as "outdoor classrooms" in which to educate and train its officers. Employing a methodology developed at Fort Leavenworth, Kansas, in 1906, both the U.S. Army Command and General Staff College and US Army War College conducted numerous battlefield staff rides to prepare officers for duties in both war and peace. Often interrupted by the exigencies of the nation's wars, the tradition was renewed and reinvigorated at Fort Leavenworth in the early 1980s. Since 1983 the Leavenworth Staff Ride Team has guided military students on battlefields around the world. For those unable to avail themselves directly of the team's services the Combat Studies Institute has begun to produce a series of staff ride guides to serve in lieu of a Fort Leavenworth instructor. The newest volume in that series, Lieutenant Colonel Jeffrey Gudmens' *Staff Ride Handbook for the Battle of Shiloh, 6-7 April 1862* is a valuable study that examines the key considerations in planning and executing the campaign and battle. Modern tacticians and operational planners will find themes that still resonate. Gudmens demonstrates that leaders in Blue and Gray, in facing the daunting tasks of this, the bloodiest battle to this point on the continent, rose to the challenge. They were able to meet this challenge through planning, discipline, ingenuity, leadership, and persistence—themes worthy of reflection by today's leaders.

Thomas T. Smith
Lieutenant Colonel, Infantry
Director of Combat Studies

# Introduction

A staff ride to a major battlefield is an excellent tool for the historical education of members of the Armed Forces. Fort Leavenworth, Kansas, has been conducting staff rides since the 1900s. Captain Arthur L. Wagner was an instructor at Fort Leavenworth in the 1890s, and he believed an officer's education had become too far removed from the reality of war. He pondered how to get the experience of combat to officers who had only experienced peace. His answer was the staff ride, a program in which students studied a major battle and then went to the actual field to complete the study. Wagner did not live to see staff rides added to the curriculum at Fort Leavenworth, but in 1906, the first staff ride was added to the Fort Leavenworth "experience." Major Eben Swift led 12 students on a study of the Atlanta Campaign of 1864. On and off, staff rides have been a part of the curriculum ever since.

Staff rides are not just limited to schoolhouse education. For years, unit commanders have conducted numerous staff rides to varied battlefields as part of their officers' and soldiers' professional development. In support of these field commanders, the Combat Studies Institute at Fort Leavenworth published staff ride guides to assist personnel planning and conducting staff rides worldwide.

In 2002, General John Abrams, US Army Training and Doctrine Command (TRADOC) commanding general, recognized the impact and importance of staff rides and revamped the Staff Ride Team. TRADOC assigned personnel full time to Fort Leavenworth to lead staff rides for the Army. As part of this initiative, the Staff Ride Team is also dedicated to publishing staff ride handbooks in support of the Army.

The *Staff Ride Handbook for the Battle of Shiloh, 6-7 April 1862* provides a systematic approach to the analysis of this early battle in the western theater of the American Civil War. Part I describes the organization of both armies, detailing their weapons, tactics, logistics, engineering, communications, and medical support. Part II consists of a campaign overview that allows students to understand how the armies met on the battlefield. Part III is a suggested route for conducting a staff ride at Shiloh. For each stop, or "stand," there is a set of travel directions, a description of the action that occurred there, vignettes by battle participants, a list of discussion or teaching points that a staff ride leader can explore at the stand, and a map of the battle actions.

Part IV provides information on conducting the integration phase of a staff ride. Suggested areas of discussion for use during the integration phase are included. Part V provides information on conducting a staff ride at Shiloh, including sources of assistance and logistics considerations. Appendix A provides the order of battle, including numbers engaged and casualties. Appendix B provides key participants' biographical information. Appendix C is a list of Medal of Honor recipients for actions at Shiloh. An annotated bibliography gives sources for preliminary study.

# I. Civil War Armies

## Organization

### *The US Army in 1861*

On the eve of the Civil War the Regular Army of the United States was essentially a frontier constabulary whose 16,000 officers and men were organized into 198 companies scattered across the nation at 79 different posts. At the start of the war, 183 of these companies were either on frontier duty or in transit while the remaining 15, mostly coastal artillery batteries, guarded the Canadian border and Atlantic coast or one of 23 arsenals. In 1861, this Army was under the command of Lieutenant General Winfield Scott, the 75-year-old hero of the Mexican-American War. His position as general in chief was traditional, not statutory, because Secretaries of War since 1821 had designated a general to be in charge of the field forces without formal congressional approval. The field forces were controlled through a series of geographic departments whose commanders reported directly to the general in chief. Both sides would use this frequently modified department system throughout the Civil War for administering regions under Army control.

Army administration was handled by a system of bureaus whose senior officers were, by 1860, in the twilight of long careers in their technical fields. Six of the 10 bureau chiefs were more than 70 years old. Modeled after the British system, these bureaus answered directly to the War Department and were not subject to the general in chief's orders. Predecessors of many of today's combat support and combat service support branches, the following bureaus had been established by 1861:

| | |
|---|---|
| Quartermaster | Medical |
| Ordnance | Adjutant General |
| Subsistence | Paymaster |
| Engineer | Inspector General |
| Topographic Engineer* | Judge Advocate General |

*Merged with the Engineer Bureau in 1863.

During the war Congress elevated the Office of the Provost Marshal and the Signal Corps to bureau status and created a Cavalry Bureau. Note that no operational planning or intelligence staff existed. American commanders before the Civil War had never required such a structure.

This system provided suitable civilian control and administrative support to the small field army before 1861. Ultimately the bureau system would respond effectively, if not always efficiently, to the mass mobilization required over the next four years. Indeed, it would remain essentially intact until the early 20th century. The Confederate government, forced to create an army and support organization from scratch, established a parallel structure to that of the US Army. In fact, many important figures in Confederate bureaus had served in one of the prewar bureaus.

## Raising the Armies

With the outbreak of war in April 1861, both sides faced the monumental task of organizing and equipping armies that far exceeded the prewar structure in size and complexity. The Federals maintained control of the Regular Army, and the Confederates initially created a Regular force, mostly on paper. Almost immediately the North lost many of its officers to the South, including some of exceptional quality. Of 1,108 Regular Army officers serving as of 1 January 1861, 270 ultimately resigned to join the South. Only a few hundred of the 15,135 enlisted men, however, left the ranks because the private soldiers did not have the option of resigning.

The federal government had two basic options for using the Regular Army. It could be divided into training and leadership cadre for newly formed volunteer regiments or be retained in units to provide a reliable nucleus for the Federal Army in coming battles. At the start, Scott envisioned a relatively small force to defeat the rebellion and therefore insisted that the Regulars fight as units. Although some Regular units fought well at the First Battle of Bull Run and in other battles, Scott's decision ultimately limited Regular units' impact on the war. Battle losses and disease soon thinned the ranks of Regulars, and officials could never recruit sufficient replacements in the face of stiff competition from the states that were forming volunteer regiments. By November 1864, many Regular units had been so depleted that they were withdrawn from front-line service. The war, therefore, was fought primarily with volunteer officers and men, the vast majority of whom had no previous military training or experience.

Neither side had difficulty in recruiting the numbers initially required to fill the expanding ranks. In April 1861, President Abraham Lincoln called up 75,000 men from the states' militias for three months. This figure probably represented Lincoln's informed guess as to how many troops would be needed to quell the rebellion quickly. Almost 92,000 men responded because most Northern states recruited their "organized" but untrained militia companies. At the First Battle of Bull Run in July 1861, these ill-trained, poorly equipped soldiers generally fought much better than they were led. Later, as the war began to require more manpower, the federal government set enlisted quotas through various "calls," which local districts struggled to fill. Similarly, the Confederate Congress authorized the acceptance of 100,000 one-year volunteers in March 1861. One-third of these men were under arms within a month. The southern spirit of voluntarism was so strong that possibly twice that number could have been enlisted, but sufficient arms and equipment were not then available.

As the war continued and casualty lists grew, the glory of volunteering faded, and both sides ultimately resorted to conscription to help fill the ranks. The Confederates enacted the first conscription law in American history in April 1862, followed by the federal government's own law in March 1863. Throughout these first experiments in American conscription, both sides administered the programs in less than a fair and efficient way. Conscription laws tended to exempt wealthier citizens, and initially, draftees could hire substitutes or pay commutation fees. As a result, the average conscript's health, capability, and morale were poor. Many eligible men, particularly in the South, enlisted to avoid the onus of being considered a conscript. Still, conscription or the threat of conscription ultimately helped provide a sufficient quantity of soldiers for both sides.

Conscription was never a popular program, and the North, in particular, tried several approaches to limit conscription requirements. These efforts included offering lucrative bounties, or fees paid to induce volunteers to fill required quotas. In addition, the Federals offered a series of reenlistment bonuses—money, 30-day furloughs, and an opportunity for veteran regiments to maintain their colors and be designated as "veteran" volunteer infantry regiments. The Federals also created an Invalid Corps (later renamed the Veteran Reserve Corps) of men unfit for front-line service who performed essential rear area duties. The Union also recruited almost 179,000 blacks, mostly in federally organized volunteer regiments. By February 1864, blacks were being conscripted in the North. In the South, recruiting or conscripting slaves was so politically sensitive that it was not attempted until March 1865, far too late to influence the war.

Whatever the faults of the manpower mobilization, it was an impressive achievement, particularly as a first effort on such a scale. Various enlistment figures exist, but the best estimates are that approximately 2 million men served in the Federal Army during 1861-1865. Of that number, 1 million were under arms at the end of the war. Because Confederate records are incomplete or were lost, estimates of their enlistments vary from 600,000 to more than 1.5 million. Most likely, between 750,000 and 800,000 men served in the Confederacy during the war, with a peak strength never exceeding 460,000. Perhaps the greatest legacy of the manpower mobilization efforts of both sides was the improved Selective Service System that created the American armies of World War I and World War II.

The unit structure into which the expanding armies were organized was generally the same for Federals and Confederates, reflecting the common roots for both armies. The Federals began the war with a Regular Army organized into an essentially Napoleonic, musket-equipped structure. Each of the 10 prewar infantry regiments consisted of 10 87-man companies with a maximum authorized strength of 878. At the beginning of the war, the Federals added nine Regular infantry regiments with a newer "French model" organizational structure. The new regiments contained three battalions, with a maximum authorized strength of 2,452. The new Regular battalion, with eight 100-man companies, was, in effect, equivalent to the prewar regiment. Essentially an effort to reduce staff officer slots, the new structure was unfamiliar to most leaders, and both sides used a variant of the old structure for newly formed volunteer regiments. The Federal War Department established a volunteer infantry regimental organization with a strength that could range from 866 to 1,046, varying in authorized strength by up to 180 infantry privates. The Confederate Congress fixed its 10-company infantry regiment at 1,045 men. Combat strength in battle, however, was always much lower because of casualties, sickness, leaves, details, desertions, and stragglers.

The battery remained the basic artillery unit, although battalion and larger formal groupings of artillery emerged later in the war in the eastern theater. Four understrength Regular regiments existed in the US Army at the start of the war, and one Regular regiment was added in 1861, for a total of 60 batteries. Nevertheless, most batteries were volunteer organizations. A Federal battery usually consisted of six guns and had an authorized strength of 80 to 156 men. A battery of six 12-pounder Napoleons could include 130 horses. If organized as "horse" or flying artillery, cannoneers were provided individual mounts, and more horses than men could be assigned to the battery. Their Confederate counterparts, plagued by limited ordnance and available manpower, usually operated with a four-gun battery, often with guns of mixed types and calibers. Confederate batteries seldom reached their initially authorized manning level of 80 soldiers.

Prewar Federal mounted units were organized into five Regular regiments (two dragoon, two cavalry, and one mounted rifle), and one Regular cavalry regiment was added in May 1861. Originally, 10 companies comprised a regiment, but congressional legislation in July 1862 officially reorganized the Regular mounted units into standard regiments of 12 "companies or troops" of 79 to 95 men each. Although the term "troop" was officially introduced, most cavalrymen continued to use the more familiar term "company" to describe their units throughout the war. The Federals grouped two companies or troops into squadrons, with four to six squadrons making a regiment. Confederate cavalry units, organized in the prewar model, authorized 10 76-man companies per regiment. Some volunteer cavalry units on both sides also formed into smaller cavalry battalions. Later in the war, both sides began to merge their cavalry regiments and brigades into division and corps organizations.

For both sides, unit structure above regimental level was similar to today's structure, with a brigade controlling three to five regiments and a division controlling two or more brigades. Federal brigades generally contained regiments from more than one state, while Confederate brigades often had several regiments from the same state. In the Confederate Army, a brigadier general usually commanded a brigade, and a major general commanded a division. The Federal Army, with no rank higher than major general until 1864, often had colonels commanding brigades and brigadier generals commanding divisions.

The large numbers of organizations formed, as shown in table 1, reflect the politics of the time. The War Department in 1861 considered making recruiting a federal responsibility, but this proposal seemed to be an unnecessary expense for the short war initially envisioned. Therefore, responsibility for recruiting remained with the states, and on both sides, state governors continually encouraged local constituents to form new volunteer regiments. This practice strengthened support for local, state, and national politicians and provided an opportunity for glory and high rank for ambitious men. Although such local recruiting created regiments with strong bonds among the men, it hindered filling the ranks of existing regiments with new replacements. As the war progressed, the Confederates attempted to funnel replacements into units from their same state or region, but the Federals continued to create new regiments. Existing Federal regiments detailed men back home to recruit replacements, but these efforts could never successfully compete for men joining new local regiments. The newly formed regiments thus had no seasoned veterans to train the recruits, and the battle-tested regiments lost men faster than they could recruit replacements. Many regiments on both sides were reduced to combat ineffectiveness as the war progressed. Seasoned regiments were often disbanded or consolidated, usually against the wishes of the men assigned.

Table 1. Federal and Confederate Organized Forces

| | Federal | | Confederate | |
|---|---|---|---|---|
| Infantry | 19 | regular regiments | 642 | regiments |
| | 2,125 | volunteer regiments | 9 | legions* |
| | 60 | volunteer battalions | 163 | separate battalions |
| | 351 | separate companies | 62 | separate companies |
| Artillery | 5 | regular regiments | 16 | regiments |
| | 61 | volunteer regiments | 25 | battalions |
| | 17 | volunteer battalions | 227 | batteries |
| | 408 | separate batteries | | |
| Cavalry | 6 | regular regiments | 137 | regiments |
| | 266 | volunteer regiments | 1 | legion* |
| | 45 | battalions | 143 | separate battalions |
| | 78 | separate companies | 101 | separate companies |

*Legions were a form of combined arms team with artillery, cavalry, and infantry units. They were approximately the strength of a large regiment. Long before the end of the war, legions lost their combined arms organization.

## The Leaders

Because the Confederate and Federal Armies' organization, equipment, tactics, and training were similar, units' performance in battle often depended on the quality and performance of their individual leaders. General officers were appointed by their respective central governments. At the start of the war, most, but certainly not all, of the more senior officers had West Point or other military school experience. In 1861, Lincoln appointed 126 general officers, of which 82 were or had been professional officers. Jefferson Davis appointed 89, of which 44 had received professional training. The remaining officers were political appointees, but of those only 16 Federal and seven Confederate generals had no military experience.

Of the volunteer officers who composed most of the leadership for both armies, colonels (regimental commanders) were normally appointed by state governors. Other field grade officers were appointed by their states, although many were initially elected within their units. The men usually elected their company grade officers. This long-established militia tradition, which seldom made military leadership and capability a primary consideration, was largely an extension of the states' rights philosophy and sustained political patronage in both the Union and the Confederacy.

Much has been made of the West Point backgrounds of the men who ultimately dominated the senior leadership positions of both armies, but the graduates of military colleges were not prepared by such institutions to command divisions, corps, or armies. Moreover, although many leaders had some combat experience from the Mexican War era, very few had experience above the company or battery level in the peacetime years before 1861. As a result, the war was not initially conducted at any level by "professional officers" in today's terminology. Leaders became more professional through experience and at the cost of thousands of lives. General William T. Sherman would later note that the war did not enter its "professional stage" until 1863.

## Civil War Staffs

In the Civil War, as today, large military organizations' success often depended on the effectiveness of the commanders' staffs. Modern staff procedures have evolved only gradually with the increasing complexity of military operations. This evolution was far from complete in 1861, and throughout the war, commanders personally handled many vital staff functions, most notably operations and intelligence. The nature of American warfare up to the mid-19th century had not yet clearly overwhelmed single commanders' capabilities.

Civil War staffs were divided into a "general staff" and a "staff corps." This terminology, defined by Scott in 1855, differs from modern definitions of the terms. Table 2 lists typical staff positions at army level, although key functions are represented down to regimental level. Except for the chief of staff and aides-de-camp, who were considered personal staff and would often depart when a commander was reassigned, staffs mainly

### Table 2. Typical Staffs

| | |
|---|---|
| General Staff | Chief of Staff |
| | Aides |
| | Assistant Adjutant General |
| | Assistant Inspector General |
| | |
| Staff Corps | Engineer |
| | Ordnance |
| | Quartermaster |
| | Subsistence |
| | Medical |
| | Pay |
| | Signal |
| | Provost Marshal |
| | Chief of Artillery |

contained representatives of the various bureaus, with logistical areas being best represented. Later in the war, some truly effective staffs began to emerge, but this was a result of the increased experience of the officers serving in those positions rather than a comprehensive development of standard staff procedures or guidelines.

George B. McClellan, when he appointed his father-in-law as his chief of staff, was the first American to use this title officially. Even though many senior commanders had a chief of staff, the position was not used in any uniform way and seldom did the man in this role achieve the central coordinating authority of the chief of staff in modern headquarters. This position, along with most other staff positions, was used as an individual commander saw fit, making staff responsibilities somewhat different under each commander. This inadequate use of the chief of staff was among the most important shortcomings of staffs during the Civil War. An equally important weakness was the lack of any formal operations or intelligence staff. Liaison procedures were also ill defined, and various staff officers or soldiers performed this function with little formal guidance. Miscommunication or lack of knowledge of friendly units proved disastrous time after time.

*The Armies at Shiloh*

MG Henry Halleck assumed command of the newly created US Department of the Mississippi on 11 March 1862. He was responsible for the territory from the Mississippi River east to the Appalachian Mountains. With headquarters in St. Louis, Halleck had three field armies in his department: the Army of the Tennessee under the command of Major General (MG) Ulysses S. Grant, the Army of the Ohio under MG Don Carlos Buell, and the Army of the Mississippi under MG John Pope. Only Grant and Buell would see action at Shiloh; Pope would campaign against Island No. 10.

Grant's Army of the Tennessee was organized into six divisions with a strength of 48,000 troops. The army was a mixed bag of veteran units and "green" units. The experienced troops were veterans of the battles of Fort Donelson and Fort Henry. MG John A. McClernand, a general who had been a Democratic Congressman before the war, commanded the 1st Division. By April 1862, McClernand was the ranking division commander in the Army of the Tennessee, and Grant had concerns about his abilities and did not want him in command in his absence. The 1st Division contained 7,000 Illinois and Iowa veteran troops in three brigades. Brigadier General (BG) William Harvey Lamb Wallace commanded the

2d Division. Wallace had been a brigade commander under McClernand at Fort Donelson and had only assumed command of the 2d Division on 22 March 1862 when MG Charles F. Smith was injured. The 2d Division contained 8,500 veterans also from Illinois and Iowa in three brigades.

MG Lewis Wallace commanded the 3d Division. Wallace had fought in the Mexican War and had seen action in western Virginia and at Fort Donelson. The 3d Division contained 7,500 veterans in three brigades from mainly Ohio and Indiana. BG Stephen A. Hurlbut commanded the 4th Division. Hurlbut was an Illinois politician known for hard drinking and questionable business deals. The 4th Division, a mix of veterans and inexperienced troops, contained 6,500 men in three brigades from Illinois, Iowa, Indiana, and Kentucky. BG William T. Sherman commanded the 5th Division. Sherman was the only West Point graduate division commander in Grant's army. Sherman had fought at 1st Bull Run and had been relieved of command earlier in the war when many considered him crazy. The 5th Division was a new division that had 8,500 green troops, mostly Ohio men in four brigades. BG Benjamin Prentiss commanded Grant's final division, the 6th. Prentiss was an Illinois lawyer with little military experience. He had feuded with Grant in 1861 over his date of rank, and their relationship was strained. The 6th Division was organized on 22 March 1862 and contained 4,000 inexperienced troops in two brigades.

Buell brought four divisions of 18,000 men of the Army of the Ohio to Shiloh. BG Alexander McCook, of the famous Ohio "Fighting McCooks," commanded the 7,500-man 2d Division. BG William "Bull" Nelson had 4,500 men in his 4th Division. The 5th Division was commanded by BG Thomas Crittenden and had 4,000 troops. BG T.J. Wood had 2,000 men in the 6th Division.

General Albert Sidney Johnston was the commander of the Confederate Army of the Mississippi, and General Pierre Gustave Toutant Beauregard was his second in command. The two enjoyed a professional relationship, but their command system can best be described as "co-command." When the Confederacy abandoned its cordon defense scheme in the west and decided to mass at Corinth, the Army of the Mississippi grew with the addition of troops from all over the South. Beauregard had 11,000 men in the vicinity of Corinth, and Johnston brought 17,000 from Murfreesboro. MG Braxton Bragg brought 10,000 men from the defenses of Pensacola and Mobile. BG Daniel Ruggles brought 5,000 men from New Orleans. When concentrated, the Army of the Mississippi had 46,000 men, the vast majority of whom were untested in battle. In March, Johnston and Beauregard organized the army into four corps.

MG Leonidas Polk commanded the I Corps. Polk was known as the "Bishop General" because he had resigned his commission 6 months after graduating from West Point to enter the ministry, eventually rising to Missionary Bishop of the Southwest. The I Corps had 9,100 men in two divisions. The II Corps fell under the command of MG Braxton Bragg. Bragg was a West Point graduate who thus far had spent the war in charge of defending Pensacola and Mobile. His corps was the largest in the army, 14,000 men in two divisions. Interestingly, Bragg was also appointed the army's chief of staff in addition to being one of its corps commanders. MG William J. Hardee commanded the III Corps. Hardee had graduated from West Point, and soldiers on both sides were using the manual on infantry tactics he had written for the US Army in the 1850s. The III Corps consisted of 6,700 troops in three brigades; there was no divisional structure. BG John C. Breckinridge commanded the Reserve Corps. Breckenridge had been a very successful politician, having served in both houses of the US Congress and as President James Buchanan's vice president. Like the III Corps, the Reserve Corps' 6,700 men were in three brigades with no divisional structure.

## Weapons

### Infantry

During the 1850s, in a technological revolution of major proportions, the rifle musket began to replace the relatively inaccurate smoothbore musket in ever-increasing numbers, both in Europe and America. This process, accelerated by the American Civil War, ensured that the rifled shoulder weapon would be the basic weapon infantrymen used in both the Federal and Confederate armies.

The standard and most common shoulder weapon used in the American Civil War was the Springfield .58-caliber rifle musket, models 1855, 1861, and 1863. In 1855, the US Army adopted this weapon to replace the .69-caliber smoothbore musket and the .54-caliber rifle. In appearance, the rifle musket was similar to the smoothbore musket. Both were single-shot muzzle loaders, but the new weapon's rifled bore substantially increased its range and accuracy. Claude Minié, a French Army officer, designed the rifling system the United States chose. Whereas earlier rifles fired a round, nonexpanding ball, the Minié system used a hollow-based cylindro-conoidal projectile slightly smaller than the bore that could be dropped easily into the barrel. When a fulminate of mercury percussion cap ignited the powder charge, the released propellent gases expanded the base of the bullet into the rifled grooves, giving the projectile a ballistic spin.

The model 1855 Springfield rifle musket was the first regulation arm to use the hollow-base .58-caliber Minié bullet. The slightly modified model 1861 was the principal infantry weapon of the Civil War, although two subsequent models were produced in almost equal quantities. The model 1861 was 56 inches long overall, had a 40-inch barrel, and weighed 8.75 pounds. It could be fitted with a 21-inch socket bayonet (with an 18-inch blade, 3- inch socket) and had a rear sight graduated to 500 yards. The maximum effective range of the Springfield rifle musket was approximately 500 yards, although it could kill at 1,000 yards. The round could penetrate 11 inches of white pine board at 200 yards and 3 ¼ inches at 1,000 yards, with penetration of 1 inch being considered the equivalent of disabling a human being. Range and accuracy were increased by using the new weapon, but the soldiers' vision was still obscured by the dense clouds of smoke its black powder propellant produced.

To load a muzzleloading rifle, a soldier took a paper cartridge in hand and tore the end of the paper with his teeth. Next he poured the powder down the barrel and placed the bullet in the muzzle. Then, using a metal ramrod, he pushed the bullet firmly down the barrel until seated. He then cocked the hammer and placed the percussion cap on the cone or nipple that when struck by the hammer ignited the gunpowder. The average rate of fire was three rounds per minute. A well-trained soldier could possibly load and fire four times per minute, but in the confusion of battle, the rate of fire was probably slower, perhaps two to three rounds per minute.

In addition to the Springfields, more than 100 types of muskets, rifles, rifle muskets, and rifled muskets—ranging up to .79 caliber—were used during the American Civil War. The numerous American-made weapons were supplemented early in the conflict by a variety of imported models. The best, most popular, and most numerous of the foreign weapons was the British .577-caliber Enfield rifle, model 1853, that was 54 inches long (with a 39-inch barrel), weighed 8.7 pounds (9.2 with the bayonet), could be fitted with a socket bayonet with an 18-inch blade, and had a rear sight graduated to a range of 800 yards. The Enfield design was produced in a variety of forms, both long and short barreled, by several British manu-facturers and at least one American company. Of all the foreign designs, the Enfield most closely resembled the Springfield in characteristics and capabilities. The United States purchased more than 436,000 Enfield pattern weapons during the war. Statistics on Confederate purchases are more difficult to ascertain, but a report dated February 1863 indicates that 70,980 long Enfields and 9,715 short Enfields had been delivered by that time, with another 23,000 awaiting delivery.

While the quality of imported weapons varied, experts considered the Enfields and the Austrian Lorenz rifle muskets to be very good. Some foreign governments and manufacturers took advantage of the huge initial demand for weapons by dumping their obsolete weapons on the American market. This practice was especially prevalent with some of the older smoothbore muskets and converted flintlocks. The greatest challenge, however, lay in maintaining these weapons and supplying ammunition and replacement parts for calibers ranging from .44 to .79. The quality of the imported weapons eventually improved as the procedures, standards, and purchasers' astuteness improved. For the most part the European suppliers provided needed weapons, and the newer foreign weapons were highly regarded.

All told, the United States purchased about 1,165,000 European rifles and muskets during the war, nearly all within the first two years. Of these, 110,853 were smoothbores. The remainder were primarily the French Minié rifles (44,250), Austrian model 1854s (266,294), Prussian rifles (59,918), Austrian Jagers (29,850), and Austrian Bokers (187,533). Estimates of total Confederate purchases ranged from 340,000 to 400,000. In addition to the Enfields delivered to the Confederacy (mentioned before), 27,000 Austrian rifles, 21,040 British muskets, and 2,020 Brunswick rifles were also purchased, with 30,000 Austrian rifles awaiting shipment.

Breechloaders and repeating rifles were available by 1861 and were initially purchased in limited quantities, often by individual soldiers. Generally, however, they were not issued to troops in large numbers because of technical problems (poor breech seals, faulty ammunition), fear by the Ordnance Department that the troops would waste ammunition, and the cost of production. The most famous of the breechloaders was the single-shot Sharps, produced in both carbine and rifle models. The model 1859 rifle was .52 caliber, 47 ⅛ inches long, weighing 8 ¾ pounds, while the carbine was .52 caliber, 39 ⅛ inches long, weighing 7 ¾ pounds. Both weapons used a linen cartridge and a pellet primer feed mechanism. Most Sharps carbines were issued to Federal cavalry units.

The best known of the repeaters was probably the seven-shot, .52-caliber Spencer that also came in both rifle and carbine models. The rifle was 47 inches long and weighed 10 pounds, while the carbine was 39 inches long and weighed 8 ¼ pounds. The first mounted infantry unit to use Spencer repeating rifles in combat was Colonel (COL) John T. Wilder's "Lightning Brigade" on 24 June 1863 at Hoover's Gap, Tennessee. The Spencer was also the first weapon the US Army adopted that fired a metallic rim-fire, self-contained cartridge. Soldiers loaded rounds through an opening in the butt of the stock that fed into the chamber through a tubular magazine by the action of the trigger guard. The hammer still had to be cocked manually before each shot.

Better than either the Sharps or the Spencer was the Henry rifle. Never adopted by the US Army in large quantity, soldiers privately purchased them during the war. The Henry was a 16-shot, .44-caliber rimfire cartridge repeater. It was 43 ½ inches long and weighed 9 ¼ pounds. The tubular magazine located directly beneath the barrel had a 15-round capacity with an additional round in the chamber. Of the approximate 13,500 Henrys produced, probably 10,000 saw limited service. The government purchased only 1,731.

The Colt repeating rifle (or revolving carbine), model 1855, also was available to Civil War soldiers in limited numbers. The weapon was produced in several lengths and calibers. The lengths varied from 32 to 42 ½ inches, while the calibers were .36, .44, and .56. The .36 and .44 calibers were made to chamber six shots, while the .56-caliber had five chambers. The Colt Firearms Company was also the primary supplier of revolvers. The .44-caliber Army revolver and the .36-caliber Navy revolver were the most popular (more than 146,000 purchased) because they were simple, sturdy, and reliable.

*Cavalry*

Initially armed with sabers and pistols (and in one case, lances), Federal cavalry troops quickly added the breechloading carbine to their inventory of weapons. However, one Federal regiment, the 6th Pennsylvania Cavalry, carried lances until 1863. Troopers preferred the easier-handling carbines to rifles and the breechloaders to awkward muzzleloaders. Of the single-shot breechloading carbines that saw extensive use during the Civil War, the Hall .52-caliber accounted for approximately 20,000 in 1861. The Hall was quickly replaced by a variety of carbines, including the Merrill .54 caliber (14,495), Maynard .52 caliber (20,002), Gallager .53 caliber (22,728), Smith .52 caliber (30,062), Burnside .56 caliber (55,567), and Sharps .54 caliber (80,512).

The next step in the evolutionary process was the repeating carbine. The favorite by 1865 was the Spencer .52-caliber, seven-shot repeater (94,194). Because of the South's limited industrial capacity, Confederate cavalrymen had a more difficult time arming themselves. Nevertheless, they too embraced the firepower revolution, choosing shotguns, muzzleloading carbines, and numerous revolvers as their primary weapons. In addition, Confederate cavalrymen made extensive use of battlefield salvage by recovering Federal weapons. However, the South's difficulties in producing the metallic-rimmed cartridges many of these recovered weapons required limited their usefulness.

*Field Artillery*

In 1841 the US Army selected bronze as the standard material for fieldpieces and at the same time adopted a new system of field artillery. The 1841 field artillery system consisted entirely of smoothbore muzzle-loaders: 6- and 12-pound guns; 12-, 24-, and 32-pound howitzers; and 12-pound mountain howitzers. A pre-Civil War battery usually consisted of six fieldpieces—four guns and two howitzers. A 6-pounder battery contained four 6-pound guns and two 12-pound howitzers, while a 12-pounder battery had four 12-pound guns and two 24-pound howitzers. The guns fired solid shot, shell, spherical case, grapeshot, and canister rounds, while howitzers fired shell, spherical case, grapeshot, and canister rounds.

The 6-pound gun (effective range of 1,523 yards) was the primary fieldpiece used from the Mexican War until the Civil War. By 1861, however, the 1841 system based on the 6-pounder was obsolete. In 1857, a new and more versatile fieldpiece, the 12-pound gun-howitzer (Napoleon), model 1857, appeared on the scene. Designed as a multipurpose piece to replace existing guns and howitzers, the Napoleon fired canisters and shells like the 12-pound howitzer and solid shot at ranges comparable to the 12-pound gun. The Napoleon was a bronze, muzzleloading smoothbore with an effective range of 1,680 yards using solid shot (see table 3 for a comparison of artillery data). Served by a nine-man crew, the piece could fire at a sustained rate of two aimed shots per minute. With less than 50 Napoleons initially available in 1861, obsolete 6-pounders remained in the inventories of both armies for some time, especially in the western theater.

Another new development in field artillery was the introduction of rifling. Although rifled guns provided greater range and accuracy, they were somewhat less reliable and slower to load than smoothbores. (Rifled ammunition was semifixed, so the charge and the projectile had to be loaded separately.) Moreover, the canister load of the rifle did not perform as well as the smoothbore. Initially, some smoothbores were rifled on the James pattern, but they soon proved unsatisfactory because the bronze rifling eroded too quickly. Therefore, most rifled artillery was wrought iron or cast iron with a wrought iron reinforcing band encircling the breach area.

The most common rifled guns were the 10-pound Parrott and the Rodman, or 3-inch ordnance rifle. The Parrott rifle was a cast-iron piece, easily identified by the wrought-iron band reinforcing the breech. The 10-pound Parrott was made in two models: the model 1861 had a 2.9-inch rifled bore with three lands and grooves and a slight muzzle swell, while the model 1863 had a 3-inch bore and no muzzle swell. The Rodman, or ordnance rifle, was a long-tubed, wrought-iron piece that had a 3-inch bore with seven lands and grooves. Ordnance rifles were sturdier than the 10-pound Parrott and displayed superior accuracy and reliability.

By 1860 the ammunition for field artillery consisted of four general types for both smoothbores and rifles: solid shot, shell, case, and canister. Solid shot for smoothbores was a round cast-iron projectile; for rifled guns it was an elongated projectile known as a bolt. Solid shot, with its smashing or battering effect, was used in a counterbattery role or against buildings and massed troop formations. The rifle's conical-shaped bolt lacked the effectiveness of the smoothbore's cannonball because it tended to bury itself upon impact instead of bounding along the ground like round shot.

Shell, also known as common or explosive shell, whether spherical or conical, was a hollow projectile filled with an explosive charge of black powder detonated by a fuse. Shell was designed to break into jagged pieces, producing an antipersonnel effect, but the low-order detonation seldom produced more than three to five fragments. In addition to its casualty-producing effects, shell had a psychological impact when it exploded over troops' heads. It was also used against field fortifications and in a counterbattery role. Case or case shot for both smoothbore and rifled guns was a hollow projectile with thinner walls than shell. The projectile was filled with round lead or iron balls set in a matrix of sulfur that surrounded a small bursting charge. Case was primarily used in an antipersonnel role. Henry Shrapnel, a British artillery officer, invented this type of round, hence the term "shrapnel."

Finally there was canister, probably the most effective round and the round of choice at close range (400 yards or less) against massed troops. Canister was essentially a tin can filled with iron balls packed in sawdust with no internal bursting charge. When fired, the can disintegrated, and the balls followed their own paths to the target. The canister round for the 12-pound Napoleon consisted of 27 1 ½-inch iron balls packed inside an elongated tin cylinder. At extremely close ranges of 200 yards or less, artillerymen often loaded double charges of canister.

## Heavy Artillery—Siege and Seacoast

The 1841 artillery system listed eight types of siege artillery and another six types as seacoast artillery. The 1861 *Ordnance Manual* included

11 different kinds of siege ordnance. The principal siege weapons in 1861 were the 4.5-inch rifle; 18- and 24-pound guns; a 24-pound howitzer and two types of 8-inch howitzer; and several types of 8- and 10-inch mortars. The normal rate of fire for siege guns and mortars was about 12 rounds per hour, but with a well-drilled crew, this could probably be increased to about 20 rounds per hour. The rate of fire for siege howitzers was somewhat lower, being about eight shots per hour.

The carriages for siege guns and howitzers were longer and heavier than field artillery carriages but were similar in construction. The model 1839 24-pounder was the heaviest piece that could be moved over the roads of the day. Alternate means of transport, such as railroad or watercraft, were required to move larger pieces any great distance.

The rounds that siege artillery fired were generally the same as those field artillery fired except that siege artillery continued to use grapeshot after it was discontinued in the field artillery (1841). A "stand of grape" consisted of nine iron balls ranging from 2 to about 3 ½ inches in diameter, depending on gun caliber.

The largest and heaviest artillery pieces in the Civil War era belonged to the seacoast artillery. These large weapons were normally mounted in fixed positions. The 1861 system included five types of columbiads ranging from 8- to 15-inch; 32- and 42-pound guns; 8- and 10-inch howitzers; and mortars of 10 and 13 inches.

Wartime additions to the Federal seacoast artillery inventory included Parrott rifles ranging from 6.4-inch to 10-inch (300-pounder). New columbiads, developed by ordnance Lieutenant Thomas J. Rodman, included 8-inch, 10-inch, and 15-inch models. The Confederates produced some new seacoast artillery of their own—Brooke rifles in 6.4- and 7-inch versions. They also imported weapons from England, including 7- and 8-inch Armstrong rifles, 6.3- to 12.5-inch Blakely rifles, and 5-inch Whitworth rifles.

Seacoast artillery fired the same projectiles as siege artillery, but with one addition—hot shot. As its name implies, hot shot was solid shot heated in special ovens until red-hot, then *carefully* loaded and fired as an incendiary round.

## Weapons at Shiloh

Neither side fought the Battle of Shiloh with its soldiers armed with the most modern weapons available. In one of the few times during the American Civil War, the Union did not enjoy an advantage of superior

Table 3. Common Types of Artillery Available at the Battle of Shiloh

**Field Artillery**

| Type | Model | Bore Diameter (inches) | Tube Length Overall (inches) | Tube Weight (pounds) | Carriage Weight (pounds) | Range (yards)/ degrees elevation |
|---|---|---|---|---|---|---|
| **Smoothbore** | | | | | | |
| 6-pound | Gun | 3.67 | 65.6 | 884 | 900 | 1,523/5° |
| 12-pound "Napoleon" | Gun-Howitzer | 4.62 | 72.15 | 1,227 | 1,128 | 1,680/5° |
| 12-pound | Howitzer | 4.62 | 58.6 | 788 | 900 | 1,072/5° |
| 24-pound | Howitzer | 5.82 | 71.2 | 1,318 | 1,128 | 1,322/5° |
| **Rifle** | | | | | | |
| 10-pound | Parrott | 3.0 | 78 | 890 | 900 | 2,970/10° |
| 3-inch | Ordnance | 3.0 | 73.3 | 820 | 900 | 2,788/10° |
| 20-pound | Parrott | 3.67 | 89.5 | 1,750 | | 4,400/15° |

infantry weapons. Most of the Union soldiers were armed with either the US model 1841 rifled musket (.69 caliber) or the US model 1842 smoothbore musket (.69 caliber). Some entire regiments were outfitted with modern weapons like the US model 1855 Springfield rifle (.58 caliber) or the imported British Enfield rifle (.577 caliber).

The Confederates were armed with an assortment of weapons. Some regiments had a combination of many different weapons. Most Confederate soldiers were armed with obsolete weapons, smoothbores and flintlocks converted to percussion cap. Some units were even armed with hunting rifles. The Army of the Mississippi had approximately 4,000 Enfield rifles that had come through the blockade and were shipped west in November 1861. Following the assault on the Hornet's Nest, the Confederates increased the total number of Enfields in the army. Two regiments immediately swapped their old weapons for Enfield rifles that Union troops surrendered.

The Union and Confederate forces had artillery parity at Shiloh; Grant had 119 cannon and Johnston had 117. Union forces organized their artillery differently in each division. Some brigades had an artillery battery, but in four of the six divisions in the Army of the Tennessee, the artillery was informally consolidated at division level. Each Confederate brigade at Shiloh had at least one artillery battery assigned; MG Patrick R. Cleburne's brigade had an entire battalion of artillery. While artillery weapons had been modernized in the east, the new pieces had not reached the western armies at Shiloh. Half of the Union artillery weapons were "leftovers" from the 1841 system, while more than 80 percent of the Confederate cannon were out of date. There was no formal artillery command and control function for either side. The infantry commanders controlled their own artillery or left its employment up to the battery officers. This made massing artillery fires difficult. Massed fires of more than 25 cannon only occurred three times during the battle.

Two of the massed artillery firings proved decisive: Ruggles' bombardment at the Hornet's Nest and Grant's last line at Pittsburg Landing. The artillery officers for each side were inexperienced and attempted to use antiquated Napoleonic tactics. On occasion, artillery went into battle within 400 yards of the enemy with the intent of firing canister. As they unlimbered their pieces, they were cut to pieces by the shoulder weapons the infantryman carried. Artillerymen suffered heavy casualties at Shiloh. The Union artillery lost 32 killed, 245 wounded, and four missing. The Confederates had 40 artillerymen killed, 169 wounded, and five missing. The naval gunfire support from the USS *Tyler* and the USS *Lexington* was effective and more than likely influenced Beauregard's decision to stop the battle on the first day. The fire from their 32-pound and 8-inch guns caused some casualties, but the psychological effect was substantially greater.

## Tactics

### *Tactical Doctrine in 1861*

The Napoleonic Wars and the Mexican War were the major influences on American tactical thinking at the beginning of the Civil War. The campaigns of Napoleon Bonaparte and the Duke of Wellington provided ample lessons in battle strategy, weapons employment, and logistics, while American tactical doctrine reflected the lessons learned in Mexico (1846-48). However, these tactical lessons were misleading because in Mexico relatively small armies fought only seven pitched battles. Because these battles were so small, almost all the tactical lessons learned during the war focused at the regiment, battery, and squadron levels. Future Civil War leaders had learned very little about brigade, division, and corps maneuver in Mexico, yet these units were the basic fighting elements of both armies in 1861-65.

The US Army's experience in Mexico validated Napoleonic principles—particularly that of the offensive. In Mexico, tactics did not differ greatly from those of the early 19th century. Infantry marched in columns and deployed into lines to fight. Once deployed, an infantry regiment might send one or two companies forward as skirmishers, as security against surprise, or to soften the enemy's line. After identifying the enemy's position, a regiment advanced in closely ordered lines to within 100 yards. There it delivered a devastating volley, followed by a charge with bayonets. Both sides used this basic tactic in the first battles of the Civil War.

In Mexico, American armies employed artillery and cavalry in both offensive and defensive battle situations. In the offense, artillery moved as near to the enemy lines as possible—normally just outside musket range of about 200 yards—to blow gaps in the enemy's line that the infantry might exploit with a determined charge. In the defense, artillery blasted advancing enemy lines with canister and withdrew if the enemy attack got within musket range. Cavalry guarded the Army's flanks and rear but held itself ready to charge if enemy infantry became disorganized or began to withdraw.

These tactics worked perfectly well with the weapons technology of the Napoleonic and Mexican wars. The infantry musket was accurate up to 100 yards but ineffective against even massed targets beyond that range. Rifles were specialized weapons with excellent accuracy and range but slow to load and therefore not usually issued to line troops. Smoothbore cannon had a range up to 1 mile with solid shot but were most effective against infantry when firing canister at ranges under 400 yards. Artillerists worked their guns without much fear of the infantry muskets' limited range. Cavalry continued to use sabers and lances as shock weapons.

American troops took the tactical offensive in most Mexican War battles with great success, and they suffered fairly light losses. Unfortunately, similar tactics proved to be obsolete in the Civil War because of a major technological innovation fielded in the 1850s—the cylindro-conoidal rifle musket. This new weapon greatly increased the infantry's range and accuracy and loaded as fast as a musket. The US Army adopted a version of the rifle musket in 1855, and by the beginning of the Civil War, rifle muskets were available in moderate numbers. It was the weapon of choice in both the Union and Confederate Armies during the war, and by 1862, large numbers of troops on both sides had good-quality rifle muskets.

Official tactical doctrine before the beginning of the Civil War did not clearly recognize the potential of the new rifle musket. Before 1855 the most influential tactical guide was MG Winfield Scott's three-volume work, *Infantry Tactics* (1835), based on French tactical models of the Napoleonic Wars. It stressed close-order, linear formations in two or three ranks advancing at "quick time" of 110 steps (86 yards) per minute. In 1855, to accompany the introduction of the new rifle musket, Major

William J. Hardee published a two-volume tactical manual, *Rifle and Light Infantry Tactics*. Hardee's work contained few significant revisions of Scott's manual. His major innovation was to increase the speed of the advance to a "double-quick time" of 165 steps (151 yards) per minute. If, as suggested, Hardee introduced his manual as a response to the rifle musket, then he failed to appreciate the weapon's impact on combined arms tactics and the essential shift the rifle musket made in favor of the defense. Hardee's *Tactics* was the standard infantry manual both sides used at the outbreak of war in 1861.

If Scott's and Hardee's works lagged behind technological innovations, at least the infantry had manuals to establish a doctrinal basis for training. Cavalry and artillery fell even farther behind in recognizing the potential tactical shift in favor of rifle-armed infantry. The cavalry's manual, published in 1841, was based on French sources that focused on close-order offensive tactics. It favored the traditional cavalry attack in two ranks of horsemen armed with sabers or lances. The manual took no notice of the rifle musket's potential, nor did it give much attention to dismounted operations. Similarly, the artillery had a basic drill book delineating individual crew actions, but it had no tactical manual. Like cavalrymen, artillerymen showed no concern for the potential tactical changes the rifle musket implied.

Regular Army infantry, cavalry, and artillery troops practiced and became proficient in the tactics that brought success in Mexico. As the first volunteers drilled and readied themselves for the battles of 1861, officers and noncommissioned officers taught the lessons learned from the Napoleonic Wars that were validated in Mexico. Thus, the two armies entered the Civil War with a good understanding of the tactics that had worked in the Mexican War but with little understanding of how the rifle musket might upset their carefully practiced lessons.

## Early War Tactics

In the battles of 1861 and 1862, both sides employed the tactics proven in Mexico and found that the tactical offensive could still be successful—but only at a great cost in casualties. Men wielding rifled weapons in the defense generally ripped frontal assaults to shreds, and if the attackers paused to exchange fire, the slaughter was even greater. Rifles also increased the relative numbers of defenders since flanking units now engaged assaulting troops with a murderous enfilading fire. Defenders usually crippled the first assault line before a second line of attackers could come forward in support. This caused successive attacking lines to intermingle with survivors to their front, thereby destroying formations, command, and control. Although both sides favored the bayonet throughout the war, they quickly discovered that rifle musket fire made successful bayonet attacks almost impossible.

Just as infantry troops found the bayonet charge to be of little value against rifle muskets, cavalry and artillery troops made troubling discoveries of their own. Cavalry troops soon learned that the old-style saber charge did not work against infantry troops armed with rifle muskets. Cavalry troops, however, retained their traditional intelligence-gathering and screening roles whenever commanders chose to make the horsemen the "eyes and ears" of the Army. Artillery troops found that they could not maneuver freely to canister range as they had in Mexico because the rifle musket was accurate beyond that distance. Worse yet, at ranges where gunners were safe from rifle fire, artillery shot, shell, and case were far less effective than close-range canister. Ironically, rifled cannon did not give the equivalent boost to artillery effectiveness that the rifle musket gave to the infantry. The cannons' increased range proved to be no real advantage in the broken and wooded terrain over which so many Civil War battles were fought.

There are several possible reasons why Civil War commanders continued to employ the tactical offensive long after it was clear that the defensive was superior. Most commanders believed the offensive was the decisive form of battle. This lesson came straight from the Napoleonic Wars and the Mexican-American War. Commanders who chose the tactical offensive usually retained the initiative over defenders. Similarly, the tactical defensive depended heavily on the enemy attacking at a point that was convenient to the defender and continuing to attack until badly it was defeated. Although this situation occurred often in the Civil War, a prudent commander could hardly count on it for victory. Consequently, few commanders chose to exploit the defensive form of battle if they had the option to attack.

The offensive may have been the decisive form of battle, but it was very hard to coordinate and even harder to control. The better generals often tried to attack the enemy's flanks and rear but seldom achieved success because of the difficulty involved. Not only did the commander have to identify the enemy's flank or rear correctly, he also had to move his force into position to attack and do so in conjunction with attacks that other friendly units made. Command and control of the type required to conduct these attacks was quite beyond most Civil War commanders' ability. Therefore, Civil War armies repeatedly attacked each other frontally, resulting in high casualties, because that was the easiest way to conduct offensive operations. When attacking frontally, a commander had to choose between attacking on a broad front or a narrow front. Attacking on a broad front rarely succeeded except against weak and scattered defenders. Attacking on a narrow front promised greater success but required immediate reinforcement and continued attack to achieve decisive results. As the war dragged on, attacking on narrow fronts against specific objectives became a standard tactic that fed ever-growing casualty lists.

## Later War Tactics

Poor training may have contributed to high casualty rates early in the war, but casualties remained high and even increased long after the armies became experienced. Continued high casualty rates resulted because tactical developments failed to adapt to new weapons technology. Few commanders understood how the rifle musket strengthened the tactical defensive. However, some commanders made offensive innovations that met with varying success. When an increase in the speed of the advance did not overcome defending firepower (as Hardee suggested it would), some units tried advancing in more open order. But this sort of formation lacked the appropriate mass to assault and carry prepared positions and created command and control problems beyond the Civil War leaders' ability to resolve. Late in the war, when the difficulty of attacking field fortifications under heavy fire became apparent, other tactical expedients were employed. Attacking solidly entrenched defenders often required whole brigades and divisions moving in dense masses to rapidly cover intervening ground, seize the objective, and prepare for the inevitable counterattack. Seldom successful against alert and prepared defenses, these attacks were generally accompanied by tremendous casualties and foreshadowed the massed infantry assaults of World War I.

Sometimes large formations attempted mass charges over short distances without halting to fire. This tactic enjoyed limited success at Spotsylvania Court House in May 1864. At Spotsylvania, a Union division attacked and captured an exposed portion of the Confederate line. The attack succeeded because the Union troops crossed the intervening ground very quickly without artillery preparation and without stopping to fire their rifles. Once inside the Confederate defenses, the Union troops attempted to exploit their success by continuing their advance, but loss of command and control rendered them little better than a mob. Counterattacking Confederate units in conventional formations eventually forced the Federals to relinquish much of the ground they had gained.

As the war dragged on, tactical maneuver focused more on larger formations—brigade, division, and corps. In most of the major battles fought after 1861, brigades were employed as the primary maneuver formations, but brigade maneuver was at the upper limit of command and control for most Civil War commanders. Brigades might have been able to retain coherent formations if the terrain had been suitably open, but most often, brigade attacks degenerated into a series of poorly coordinated regimental lunges through broken and wooded terrain. Thus, brigade commanders were often on the main battle line trying to influence regimental fights. Typically, defending brigades stood in the line of battle and blazed away at attackers as rapidly as possible. Volley fire usually did not continue beyond the first round. Most of the time soldiers fired as soon as they were ready, and it was common for two soldiers to work together, one loading while the other fired. Brigades were generally invulnerable to attacks on their front and flanks if units to the left and right held their ground or if reinforcements came up to defeat the threat.

Two or more brigades constituted a division. When a division attacked, its brigades often advanced in sequence, from left to right or vice versa—depending on terrain, suspected enemy location, and number of brigades available to attack. At times divisions attacked with two or more brigades leading, followed by one or more brigades ready to reinforce the lead brigades or maneuver to the flanks. Two or more divisions constituted a corps that might conduct an attack as part of a larger plan the army commander controlled. More often, groups of divisions attacked under the control of a corps-level commander. Division and corps commanders generally took a position to the rear of the main line to control the flow of reinforcements into the battle, but they often rode forward into the battle lines to influence the action personally.

Of the three basic branches, the cavalry made the greatest adaptation during the war. It learned to use its horses for mobility, then dismount and fight on foot like the infantry. The cavalry regained a useful battlefield role by employing this dragoon tactic, especially after repeating and breechloading rifles gave it the firepower and accuracy to contend with enemy infantry troops. The cavalry also found a role off the battlefield in long-range raids that interdicted enemy supply lines and diverted enemy troops in a manner that foreshadowed air interdiction in the 20th century. The campaign for Vicksburg included two excellent examples of this function. The first was a Confederate raid on the Union supply depot at Holly Springs that MG Earl Van Dorn led in December 1862 that effectively thwarted Grant's first offensive into Mississippi. The second was a Union raid from Tennessee to Baton Rouge, Louisiana, that COL Benjamin H. Grierson led that diverted Confederate attention away from Grant's main effort in April 1863.

In contrast to the cavalry, which reasserted itself as an offensive arm, the artillery found that it could best add its firepower to the rifle musket and tip the balance even more in favor of the tactical defensive, but the artillery never regained the importance to offensive maneuver that it held in Mexico. If the artillery had developed an indirect firing system, as it did before World War I, it might have been able to contribute more to offensive tactics. Still, both sides employed artillery decisively in defensive situations throughout the war.

The most significant tactical innovation in the Civil War was the widespread use of field fortifications after armies realized the tactical offensive's heavy cost. It did not take long for the rifle musket's deadly firepower to convince soldiers to entrench every time they halted. Eventually, armies dug complete trenches within an hour of halting in a position. Within 24 hours, armies could create defensive works that were nearly impregnable to frontal assaults. In this respect, this development during the American Civil War was a clear forerunner of the kind of warfare that came to dominate World War I.

### Summary

In the Civil War, the tactical defense dominated the tactical offense because assault formations proved inferior to the defender's firepower. The rifle musket, in its many forms, provided this firepower and caused the following specific alterations in tactics during the war:

- It required the attacker, in his initial dispositions, to deploy farther away from the defender, thereby increasing the distance over which the attacker had to pass.

- It increased the number of defenders who could engage attackers (with the addition of effective enfilading fire).

- It reduced the density of both attacking and defending formations.

- It created a shift of emphasis in infantry battles toward firefights rather than shock attacks.

- It caused battles to last longer because units could not close with each other for decisive shock action.

- It encouraged the widespread use of field fortifications. Armies' habitual use of field fortifications by was a major American innovation in 19th-century warfare.

- It forced the cavalry to the battlefield's fringes until cavalrymen acquired equivalent weapons and tactics.

- It forced the artillery to abandon its basic offensive maneuver— moving forward to within canister range of defending infantry troops.

## Tactics at Shiloh

As the units of the Army of the Tennessee arrived in the vicinity of Shiloh Church and established camps, they cleared areas in large fields so they could drill. Many of the troops were untrained, and their commanders wanted to teach them the intricacies of drill on open terrain. Unfortunately, the Battle of Shiloh would not be fought on open terrain. Rather, it would be fought in the woods and thickets of western Tennessee.

The Army of the Tennessee intended to establish camps in a tactical manner. Senior commanders ordered their subordinates to establish camps that allowed troops' rapid movement into good, supported battle lines. The troops and junior leaders did not think the enemy was any closer than Corinth, so a lot of the camps were established based on good camping ground and the availability of fresh water. Senior commanders did not correct this situation.

When Johnston and Beauregard developed their plan of attack, they made it as simple as possible because they did not think their untried troops and subordinate commanders could handle intricate maneuvers. The Confederates attacked with their four corps in successive lines. Within the first two lines, the brigade commanders deployed their regiments in accordance with the procedures of Hardee's manual. All of the brigade's regiments were formed in a long line, two ranks deep. The last two lines attacked in columns of brigades. On paper, this scheme seemed easy, but the thick terrain and the soldiers' baptism of fire led to adverse results. Units in the leading corps began to splinter and become intermingled. When units from succeeding corps lines moved up to support, they added to the confusion and intermingling. Soon, commanders from brigade to corps lost control of their troops. Troops from different units became so hopelessly mixed that the corps commanders, on their own, divided the battlefield into sectors and commanded the troops within the sectors regardless of parent organization.

The frontal attack was the maneuver of choice during the Battle of Shiloh. The Confederates employed the frontal attack in assaults on Sherman and McClernand. Most of Sherman and McClernand's men were armed with antiquated weapons that did not have the extended range of the Springfield or Enfield, and they had no protection. Casualties were still very high. When the Confederates faced the men in the Hornet's Nest, the frontal attack was unsuccessful. Some of the Union soldiers were armed with modern weapons that ripped the Confederate frontal attacks apart. Other Union soldiers had the protection of fences, and the Confederates sometimes attacked across open ground. Bragg ordered eight frontal attacks against the Hornet's Nest and was not successful until artillery was massed and infantry units surrounded the Union troops.

Union soldiers defended in linear formations. The poor tactical emplacement of camps ensured that many units formed with unsupported flanks. When the Confederates attacked, their local numerical superiority allowed them to overlap the unprotected Union flanks. Once its flanks were turned, the unit usually broke and ran. When one unit broke, it exposed its neighboring unit's flank, which was easily flanked. The Confederates enjoyed early success during the battle because of their ability to mass greater numbers of men at a particular location rather than their superior tactics or leadership. During the counterattack on 7 April, Union troops formed in line and conducted their own frontal assaults. For the most part, they were able to support their flanks, and their frontal attacks were able to drive the Confederates from the field through superior numbers, not tactics.

The artillery of both sides fought with archaic tactics also. There was little artillery command structure, so infantry commanders or individual battery officers chose the tactics employed. Batteries that had time to go into action with infantry support were only dislodged at a horrible price in casualties by the attackers. Infantrymen quickly learned to shoot the battery horses to prevent the battery from withdrawing. The combination of spirited attacks and loss of horses resulted in 24 of 36 cannon being lost on the Union right on 6 April. Some artillery units attempted to conduct artillery charges, the tactic of going into battle within 400 yards of the enemy and blasting it with canister. Batteries that tried this tactic were shot to pieces.

Despite a lack of effective artillery command and control, both sides were able to mass artillery with good results. The Confederates massed 53 cannon and pounded the Hornet's Nest's defenders. Grant anchored his last line at Pittsburg Landing with 52 cannons, which helped persuade the Confederates to abandon their attack.

The cavalry of both sides played a minor role in the battle due to its organization within the armies. Grant had nine battalions and eight companies of cavalry. On 2 April he had ordered the cavalry to reorganize, assigning all of it to infantry divisions. Each division had from four companies to two battalions. On 6 April the cavalry had no patrols out because no one expected an attack. Johnston had approximately five battalions of cavalry. There was no standard organization of cavalry in the Army of the Mississippi. Some brigades had cavalry troops, while others did not. A small cavalry force remained under the Army's command. When the action was joined, the Union cavalry spent most of the battle in the rear serving as escorts and couriers. The Confederate cavalry did little more. Most of the cavalry spent the battle supporting artillery batteries. The Confederates did try mounted charges, but these attacks were usually easily repulsed and suffered high casualties. However, during the retreat from the Hornet's Nest, the 1st Mississippi Cavalry captured the entire 2d Michigan Battery as it tried to run to the Pittsburg Landing. During the night of 6 April, COL Nathan Bedford Forrest's cavalry conducted extensive reconnaissance of Pittsburg Landing. Forrest reported that the Army of the Ohio had arrived, but none of the Army's leaders would listen to his reports.

On 7 April, as the Army of the Mississippi withdrew, a small legion of infantry, artillery, and cavalry covered the retreat. Grant did not pursue in earnest until 8 April. The 4th Illinois Cavalry of Sherman's Division led a token pursuit. The Union horsemen encountered Forrest's cavalry, and Forrest sent them retreating, ensuring that the Confederate army could successfully withdraw. Legend has it that during this encounter Forrest charged the Union troops and found himself surrounded. A Union soldier shot him in the hip, but Forrest scooped up a Union soldier and used him as a shield. Once he was safe, he dropped the frightened soldier. The Confederate cavalry might have provided more support during the withdrawal, but 200 cavalrymen had been dismounted so their horses could be used to bring off captured artillery.

## Logistics Support

Victory on Civil War battlefields seldom hinged on the quality or quantity of tactical logistics. On the operational and strategic levels, however, logistics capabilities and concerns always shaped campaign plans and sometimes their outcomes. As the war lengthened, the logistics advantage shifted inexorably to the North. The Federals controlled most of the nation's financial and industrial resources, and with their ability to import any needed materials, the Federals ultimately created the best-supplied army the world had yet seen. Despite suffering from shortages of raw materials, the Confederates generated adequate ordnance but faltered gradually in their ability to acquire other war materiel. The food supply for Southern armies was often on the verge of collapse, largely because the transportation network's limitations were compounded by politico-military mismanagement. Still, the state of supply within field armies on both sides depended more on the caliber of the people managing the resources than on the constraints of the available materiel.

One of the most pressing needs at the start of the war was for sufficient infantry and artillery weapons. Large quantities of outmoded muskets were on hand for both sides, either in arsenals or private hands. The Federals initially had only 35,000 modern rifle muskets, and the Confederates had seized about 10,000 of them. Purchasing agents rushed to Europe to buy existing stocks or to contract for future production. This led to an influx of outmoded weapons that resulted in many soldiers going into battle with Mexican War-era smoothbore muskets. As late as fall 1863 soldiers on both sides in the western theater were armed with smoothbore muskets. Several of Grant's regiments in the Vicksburg Campaign noted exchanging their muskets for captured Confederate Enfields. Modern artillery pieces were generally available in adequate quantities, although the Confederates usually were outgunned. Although breech-loading technology was available and the Confederates had imported some Whitworths from England, muzzle-loading smoothbore or rifled cannon were the standard pieces both armies used.

With most of the government arsenals and private manufacturing capability located in the North, the Federals ultimately produced sufficient modern firearms for their armies, but the Confederates also accumulated adequate quantities, either from battlefield captures or through the blockade. In addition, exceptional management within the Confederate Ordnance Bureau led to the creation of a series of arsenals throughout the South that produced large quantities of munitions and weapons.

The Northern manufacturing capability eventually permitted the Federals to produce and outfit their forces with repeating arms, the best of which had been patented before 1861. Initially, however, the North's conservative Ordnance Bureau would not risk switching to a new, unproven standard weapon that could lead to soldiers wasting huge quantities of ammunition in the midst of an expanding war. By 1864, after the retirement of Chief of Ordnance James Ripley and with President Lincoln's urging, Federal cavalry received seven-shot Spencer repeating carbines that greatly increased their battle capabilities.

Both sides initially relied on the states and local districts to provide some equipment, supplies, animals, and foodstuffs. As the war progressed, more centralized control over production and purchasing emerged under both governments. Still, embezzlement and fraud were common problems for both sides throughout the war. The North, with its preponderance of railroads and developed waterways, had ample supply and adequate distribution systems. The South's major supply problem was subsistence. Arguably, the South produced enough food during the war to provide for both military and civilian needs, but mismanagement, parochial local interests, and the relatively underdeveloped transportation network often created havoc with distribution.

In both armies, the Quartermaster, Ordnance, Subsistence, and Medical Bureaus procured and distributed equipment, food, and supplies. The items for which these bureaus were responsible are not dissimilar to the classes of supply used today. Some needs overlapped, such as the Quartermaster Bureau procuring wagons for medical ambulances, but conflicts of interest usually were manageable. Department and army commanders requested needed resources directly from the bureaus, and bureau chiefs wielded considerable power as they parceled out occasionally limited resources.

When essential equipment and supplies could not be obtained through normal channels, some commanders used their own resources to procure them. One example of someone who used this practice was COL John T. Wilder, who personally contracted for Spencer rifles for his mounted brigade in the Army of the Cumberland. Wilder obtained an unsecured personal loan to purchase the weapons, and his men reimbursed him from their pay. The federal government picked up the cost after the rifles' worth was demonstrated in the Tullahoma and Chickamauga Campaigns.

Typically, materiel flowed from the factory to base depots as the responsible bureaus directed. Supplies were then shipped to advanced depots, generally a city on a major transportation artery safely within the rear area of a department. During campaigns, the armies established temporary advance depots served by rail or river transportation. From these points, wagons carried the supplies forward to the field units. This principle is somewhat similar to the modern theater sustainment organization.

Managing this logistics system was complex and crucial. A corps wagon train, if drawn by standard six-mule teams, would be spread out from 5 to 8 miles, based on the difficulty of terrain, weather, and road conditions. The wagons, which were capable of hauling 4,000 pounds in optimal conditions, could carry only half that load in difficult terrain. Sustenance for the animals was a major restriction because each animal required up to 26 pounds of hay and grain a day to stay healthy and productive. Bulky and hard to handle, forage was a major consideration in campaign planning. Wagons delivering supplies more than one day's distance from the depot could be forced to carry excessive amounts of animal forage. If full animal forage was to be carried, the required number of wagons to support a corps increased dramatically with each subsequent day's distance from the forward depot. Another problem was created by herds of beef that often accompanied the trains or were appropriated en route. This provided fresh (though tough) meat for the troops, but it slowed and complicated movement.

The bulk supply problems were alleviated somewhat by the practice of foraging, which, in the proper season, supplied much of the food for the animals and men of both sides. Foraging was practiced with and without command sanction wherever an army went, and it became command policy during Grant's Vicksburg Campaign.

Table 4. Sample of Federal Logistics Data

| Item | Packing | Weight in Pounds |
|---|---|---|
| Bulk ammunition: | | |
| .58-caliber, expanding ball (500-grain bullet) | 1,000 rounds per box | 98 |
| 12-pound Napoleon canister (14.8 lb per round) | 8 rounds per box | 161 |
| "Marching" ration (per man per day): 1 lb hard bread (hardtack) ¾ lb salt pork or ¼ lb fresh meat 1 oz coffee 3 oz sugar and salt | | 2 |
| Forage (per horse per day): 14 lb hay and 12 lb grain | | 26 |
| Personal equipment: Includes rifle, bayonet, 60 rounds of ammunition, haversack, 3 days' rations, blanket, shelter half, canteen, personal items | | 50-60 |

*Logistics at Shiloh*

Union troops depended on riverboats for most of their logistics support. The Union used 174 riverboats for transportation and supply during the campaign and battle. Riverboat operations were the purview of the Quartermaster Department of the Army, not the Navy. The Navy provided all gunboat support, but the Army controlled riverboats that were used for logistics.

The Army of the Tennessee moved from northern Tennessee to Savannah and Pittsburg Landing on riverboats, bringing all of its supplies and equipment on the boats. Due to the large number of boats, the Union soldiers enjoyed a comfortable camp life with many good tents and assorted comfort items. They had all of the required supplies on hand, but the distribution system was faulty. Due to a lack of covered storage areas, supplies remained on the boats. As items were needed, the appropriate boat landed at Pittsburg Landing and unloaded those items. The boat then left the landing and loitered in the river. This system took a long time to obtain the required items that were on hand. During the battle, Pittsburg Landing was overwhelmed with riverboats shuttling Buell's troops across the river and evacuating the wounded. As such, when units needed ammunition, it was difficult to obtain because the ammunition boats could not find berthing space at Pittsburg Landing. The ammunition was on hand, but the troops who needed it could not get it.

When the Confederates evacuated Nashville, they lost their major logistics base in the west. Nashville had many quartermaster and subsistence warehouses as well as two gunpowder mills. When the Army of the Ohio occupied Nashville, it captured vast amounts of supplies.

Johnston concentrated at Corinth because it was a rail hub. Accordingly, the Confederates were able to accumulate required supplies. Corinth became the Army of the Mississippi's base of supply. During the concentration, the Confederates sent 1,800,000 rounds of rifle ammunition and 4,000 artillery rounds to Johnston. As the Confederate troops moved to Corinth, they brought their wagons with them. The Confederacy forwarded more than 30 more complete wagons with mule teams to Johnston. (These wagons came disassembled to Corinth. By a Herculean effort, the Confederates assembled the wagons before the battle.) During the battle the Confederates captured large amounts of supplies from the Union camps. Many Confederate soldiers obtained a lot of individual equipment and luxuries while pilfering Union camps.

## Engineer Support

Engineers on both sides performed many tasks that were essential to every campaign. West Point-trained engineers were at a premium; thus, many civil engineers, commissioned as volunteers, supplemented the work that professional engineer officers did. The Confederates, in particular, relied on civilian expertise because many of their trained engineer officers sought line duties. State or even local civil engineers planned and supervised much of the work done on local fortifications.

In the prewar US Army, the Corps of Engineers contained a handful of staff officers and one company of trained engineer troops. This cadre expanded to a four-company Regular engineer battalion. Congress also created a single company of topographic engineers that joined the Regular battalion when the engineer bureaus merged in 1863. In addition, several volunteer pioneer regiments, some containing up to 2,000 men, supported the various field armies. The Corps of Engineers also initially controlled the fledgling Balloon Corps, which provided aerial reconnaissance. The Confederate Corps of Engineers, formed as a small staff and one company of sappers, miners, and pontoniers in 1861, grew more slowly and generally relied on details and contract labor rather than established units with trained engineers and craftsmen.

Engineer missions for both sides included constructing fortifications; repairing and constructing roads, bridges, and, in some cases, railroads; demolition; limited construction of obstacles; and constructing or reducing siege works. The Federal Topographic Engineers, a separate prewar bureau, performed reconnaissance and produced maps. The Confederates, however, never separated these functions in creating their Corps of Engineers. Experience during the first year of the war convinced the Federals that all engineer functions should be merged under a single corps because qualified engineer officers tended to perform all related functions. As a result, the Federals also merged the Topographic Engineers into their Corps of Engineers in March 1863.

Bridging assets included wagon-mounted pontoon trains that carried either wooden, canvas-covered, or inflatable rubber pontoon boats. Using this equipment, trained engineer troops could bridge even large rivers in a matter of hours. The most remarkable pontoon bridge of the war was the 2,200-foot bridge that Army of the Potomac engineers built in 1864 over the James River. It was one of more than three dozen pontoon bridges built to support campaigns in the east that year. In 1862, the Confederates began developing pontoon trains after they had observed their effectiveness. In fact, during the Atlanta Campaign of 1864, General Joseph Johnston had four pontoon trains available to support his army.

Both armies in every campaign of the war traveled over roads and bridges that their engineers built or repaired. Federal engineers also helped clear waterways by dredging, removing trees, or digging canals. Fixed fortifications laid out under engineer supervision played critical roles in the Vicksburg Campaign and in actions around Richmond and Petersburg. Engineers also supervised the siege works to reduce those fortifications.

While the Federal engineer effort expanded in both men and materiel as the war progressed, major problems continued to hamper the Confederate engineer efforts. The relatively small number of organized engineer units available forced Confederate engineers to rely heavily on details or contract labor. Finding adequate manpower, however, was often difficult because of competing demands for it. Local slave owners were reluctant to provide labor details when labor was crucial to their economic survival. Despite congressional authorization to conscript 20,000 slaves as a labor force, state and local opposition continually hindered efforts to draft slave labor. Another related problem concerned the value of Confederate currency. Engineer efforts required huge sums for men and materiel, yet initial authorizations were small, and although congressional appropriations grew later in the war, inflation greatly reduced the Confederates' effective purchasing power. A final problem was the simple shortage of iron resources that severely limited the Confederates' ability to increase railroad mileage or even produce iron tools.

In 1861 maps for both sides were also in short supply; for many areas in the interior, they were nonexistent. As the war progressed, the Federals developed a highly sophisticated mapping capability. Federal topographic engineers performed personal reconnaissance to develop base maps, reproduce them by several processes, and distribute them to field commanders. Photography, lithographic presses, and eventually photochemical processes enabled the Federals to reproduce maps quickly. Western armies, which usually operated far from base cities, carried equipment to reproduce maps on campaigns with their army headquarters. By 1864, annual map production exceeded 21,000 copies. Confederate topographic work never approached the Federal effort in quantity or quality. Confederate topographers initially used tracing paper to reproduce maps. Not until 1864 did the South's use of photographic methods become widespread.

*Engineers at Shiloh*

Lack of engineer support for the armies was the standard during the battle. When Buell's troops were marching to join Grant, they found the bridges destroyed at the Duck River. A small battalion of inexperienced pioneers and an infantry regiment made repairs, but it took the Army of the Ohio two weeks to cross the river. The Army of the Tennessee brought a pontoon bridge with them on riverboats, intending to use it to cross the Tennessee. It remained on the boats throughout the battle and was not laid until well after.

West Point produced military engineers, so both armies had an abundance of engineer staff officers. When MG Charles F. Smith ordered Sherman to Pittsburg Landing, he sent Lieutenant Colonel James McPherson, the army's chief engineer, with Sherman. McPherson assisted Sherman as he laid out the camps and provided valuable positioning advice that many brigade commanders ignored. McPherson also conducted many reconnaissance missions for the army.

MG Lew Wallace used his cavalry troops to reconnoiter a route from Crump's Landing to Pittsburg Landing. Once the route was selected, the troops improved the route by repairing the bridges and road where needed because engineer troops were unavailable.

The Confederates also had ample engineer staff officers. Lieutenant Colonel Jeremy Gilmer was Johnston's engineer, and he provided valuable assistance during the concentration of troops. Bragg's engineer, Captain S.H. Lockett, conducted a reconnaissance of the Union left and confirmed the Confederate plan to turn the Army of the Tennessee away from the river. Despite reporting a brigade as a division, Lockett's mission was successful.

Union troops did not entrench their positions. Sherman stated the troops did not entrench because the Confederates were not near, and entrenching discouraged the troops. The Union troops' performance would have been much more effective if they had entrenched and placed obstacles. The value of entrenchments was not learned until later in the war.

## Communications Support

Communications systems used during the Civil War consisted of line-of-sight signaling, telegraphic systems, and various forms of the time-honored courier. The telegraph mainly offered viable strategic and operational communications, line-of-sight signaling provided operational and limited tactical possibilities, and couriers were most heavily used for tactical communications.

The Federal Signal Corps was in its infancy during the Civil War; Major Albert C. Myer was appointed the first signal chief in 1860. His organization grew slowly and became officially recognized as the Signal Corps in March 1863, achieving bureau status by November of that year. Throughout the war the Federal Signal Corps remained small. Its maximum strength reached just 1,500 officers and men, most of who were on detached service with the corps. Myer also indirectly influenced the Confederate Signal Service's formation. Among the men who assisted Myer in prewar testing of his wigwag signaling system was Lieutenant E.P. Alexander. (Myer's wigwag system, patented in 1858, used five separate numbered movements of a single flag. Four number groups represented letters of the alphabet and a few simple words and phrases. The system could also be employed at night using kerosene torches.) Alexander used wigwag signals to the Confederates' advantage during the First Battle of Bull Run and later organized the Confederate Signal Corps. Officially established in April 1862, the Confederate Signal Corps was attached to the Adjutant and Inspector General Department. It attained the same size as its Federal counterpart, with nearly 1,500 men ultimately being detailed for service.

Myer also fought hard to develop a Federal field telegraph service. This field service used the Beardslee device, a magneto-powered machine operated by turning a wheel to a specific point that sent an electrical impulse that keyed the machine at the other end to the same letter. Although less reliable than the standard Morse code telegraph key, an operator could use the Beardslee with only several hours' training, and it did not require bulky batteries for a power source. Myer's field telegraph units carried equipment on wagons that enabled its operators to establish lines between field headquarters. The insulated wire used could also be hooked into existing trunk lines, thus offering the potential to extend the civilian telegraph network's reach. However, the US Military Telegraph Service maintained control over the existing fixed telegraph system. Myer lost his struggle to keep the field telegraph service under the Signal Corps when Secretary of War Edwin M. Stanton relieved Myer as the signal chief in November 1863 and placed all telegraph activity under the Military Telegraph Service.

Although the Confederate Signal Corps' visual communications capabilities were roughly equal to the Federals', Confederate field telegraph operations remained too limited to be operationally significant. The Confederates' existing telegraph lines provided strategic communications capabilities similar to the Federals', but lack of resources and factories in the South for producing wire precluded them from extending the prewar telegraph networks.

The courier system, using mounted staff officers or detailed soldiers to deliver orders and messages, remained the most viable tactical communications option short of commanders meeting face to face. Although often effective, this system was fraught with difficulties because couriers often were captured, killed, or delayed en route. Commanders sometimes misinterpreted or ignored messages, and situations often changed by the time messages were delivered. The courier system's weaknesses, though not always critical in themselves, did tend to compound commanders' errors or misjudgments during campaigns and battles.

## Communications at Shiloh

Communications, or rather a lack of communications, played a major role at Shiloh. The department commander did not join the forces in the field because of communications concerns. Halleck remained in St. Louis because he doubted his ability to communicate with Grant and Buell. He informed Washington that he would not move his headquarters until the telegraph reached Fort Henry, New Madrid, and Ironton.

Once Grant had seized Fort Donelson, he established his headquarters at Fort Henry so he would be on the Tennessee River. The telegraph lines connecting Halleck to Grant ended at Cairo, Illinois. As early as 8 March, Halleck complained to Grant that he was not being kept informed. Grant's communication with Halleck was tenuous at best. All of Grant's messages traveled by boat from Fort Henry to Cairo where they were telegraphed to Halleck in St. Louis. One problem was that the telegraph operator at Cairo was a Confederate sympathizer who had held up messages moving in both directions. Grant's lack of reporting to Halleck was one of the reasons cited when Halleck relieved Grant in March 1862.

As the Army of the Tennessee and the Army of the Ohio converged on Pittsburg Landing, communications problems hindered coordination. Once Grant was back in command of the Army of the Tennessee he moved his headquarters to Savannah, Tennessee. Messages between Grant and Halleck traveled by boat or courier to a newly created telegraph station at Fort Henry where they were transmitted to Halleck in St. Louis. Buell's main telegraph station was in Nashville. Buell stretched a telegraph line with him as he moved, and he was able to maintain reliable communications while he moved. Communication between Grant and Buell was burdensome. Grant sent messages to Fort Henry by boat or courier where they were relayed between telegraph stations until they finally reached Buell.

Messages between Buell and Grant could take four days one way. Buell complained of this so much that on 20 March Halleck sent a telegraph party to Savannah to connect Grant and Buell directly. Grant received a supply of telegraph wire on 21 March and immediately started stretching a line between Savannah and Fort Henry although the line would not be in before the start of the battle.

Grant had no tactical telegraph lines and had to rely on couriers and staff officers to send messages to subordinates. Grant moved from his headquarters in Savannah to Pittsburg Landing early on 6 April as soon as he heard the firing, using the steamer *Tigress* as a headquarters ship. On the way, as he passed Crump's Landing, he gave instructions to Lew Wallace by yelling from the side of his vessel. As soon as Grant arrived at Pittsburg Landing, he immediately dispatched his staff officers as couriers. He also used cavalrymen as couriers. Grant visited every division commander so he could talk to each face to face and size up the situation. Once that was complete, he moved back to Pittsburg Landing and established his command post.

Grant decided to send for Lew Wallace's division early during the battle on 6 April. He sent Captain A.S. Baxter, the army's quartermaster, to Crump's Landing to tell Wallace to come to the battlefield. Baxter thought a written order was needed, so Captain James Rawlins, the assistant adjutant general, drafted an order but did not sign it. The exact content of the order was lost when the order disappeared after its delivery, but it apparently gave some latitude for Wallace's route. Wallace would not reach the battlefield until 1930, and Grant dispatched a total of four staff officers to check on Wallace. Once Grant had visited the front lines he remained in his command post around Pittsburg Landing. Grant communicated with his subordinates by dispatching orderlies, staff officers, and cavalry troopers with messages.

The Army of the Ohio had better communications support than the Army of the Tennessee. In January 1862, it activated a signal detachment, something the Army of the Tennessee would not do until November. As the first of Buell's troops, Nelson's Division, arrived at Pittsburg Landing, they brought part of the signal detachment with them, and soon Nelson could communicate with Buell via flag signals. While sending messages, Lieutenant Hinson, the officer in charge of the detachment, noticed a mounted officer blocking the view. Hinson told the officer, "Git out of the way there; ain't you got no sense! Don't you see you're in the way?" The mounted officer quietly apologized and moved out of the way. The mounted officer was Grant.

The Confederates enjoyed an excellent telegraphic network as they concentrated for the battle because they used the existing civilian infrastructure, which tended to follow the rail line. The Confederates also used a system of ciphers to ensure their communications stayed protected. On 10 March, Beauregard wired Johnston with a simple alphabetic code. The day of the month a message was written indicated which letter represented "A." If a message was written on the 10th of the month, "J" would equal "A." "K" would equal "B", etc. On the 27th of the month, "A" would correspond with "C." Once Johnston arrived in Corinth, President Davis sent him a dictionary of which he had a duplicate. The two could communicate in code by citing a word's page number, column ("L" for left column, "M" for middle, and "R" for right), and number of words from the top.

Confederate tactical communication was no different than the Union's. Commanders remained close to the battlefield to observe, and they depended on staff officers and couriers to deliver instructions to subordinates who were not within close distances.

## Medical Support

Federal and Confederate medical systems followed a similar pattern. Surgeons General and medical directors for both sides had served many years in the prewar Medical Department but were hindered by an initial lack of administrative experience in handling large numbers of casualties. The state of medical science in the mid-19th century hampered them as well. Administrative procedures improved with experience, but throughout the war the simple lack of knowledge about the true causes of disease and infection led to many more deaths than direct battlefield action.

After the disaster at the Battle of First Bull Run, the Federal Medical Department established an evacuation and treatment system that surgeon Jonathan Letterman had developed. At the heart of the system were three precepts: consolidating field hospitals at division level, decentralizing medical supplies down to regimental level, and centralizing medical control of ambulances at all levels. A battle casualty evacuated from the front line normally received treatment at a regimental holding area immediately to the rear. From this point, wagons or ambulances carried wounded men to a division field hospital, normally within a mile of the battle lines. Seriously wounded men could then be further evacuated by wagon, rail, or watercraft to general hospitals located usually in towns along lines of communication in the armies' rear areas.

Although the Confederate system followed the same general principles, Confederate field hospitals were often consolidated at brigade level rather than at division level. A second difference lay in medical activities' established span of control. Unlike their Federal counterparts who controlled all medical activities within an army area, a Confederate army medical director had no control of activities beyond his own brigade or division field hospitals. A separate medical director for large hospitals was responsible for evacuation and control. In practice, both sets of medical directors resolved potential problems through close cooperation. By 1863, the Confederacy had also introduced rear area "wayside hospitals" to handle convalescents en route home on furloughs.

Procedures, medical techniques, and medical problems for both sides were virtually identical. Commanders discouraged soldiers from leaving the battle lines to escort wounded back to the rear, but such practice was common, especially in less-disciplined units. The established technique for casualty evacuation was to detail men for litter and ambulance duty. Both armies used bandsmen, among others, for this task. Casualties would move or be assisted back from the battle line where litter bearers evacuated them to field hospitals using ambulances or supply wagons. Ambulances were specially designed two- or four-wheeled carts with springs to limit jolts, but rough roads made even short trips agonizing for wounded men.

Brigade and division surgeons staffed consolidated field hospitals. Considerations for hospital sites included the availability of water, potential buildings to supplement the hospital tents, and security from enemy cannon and rifle fire. Most operations performed at field hospitals in the aftermath of battle were amputations. Approximately 70 percent of Civil War wounds occurred in the extremities, and the soft Minié ball shattered any bones it hit. Amputation was the best technique available to limit the chance of serious infection. The Federals were generally well supplied with chloroform, morphine, and other drugs, although shortages did occur on the battlefield. Confederate surgeons often lacked critical drugs and medical supplies.

## Medical Support at the Battle of Shiloh

By April 1861 the US Army Medical Department had not evolved from a system for a small peacetime army to a system to support a large field army. The Army of the Tennessee had established a large general hospital of 1,700 beds at Mound City, Illinois. There were also large general hospitals at Paducah, Louisville, Cincinnati, Evansville, New Albany, and St. Louis. The Medical Director of the Army of the Tennessee was surgeon H.S. Hewit. The Army of the Tennessee generally had a surgeon and an assistant surgeon with each regiment. The regimental surgeon's equipment consisted of one or two two-wheeled ambulances, one or two four-wheeled ambulance wagons, a medicine chest, a hospital knapsack (much like a modern aid bag), 20 blankets, two hospital tents, and three stretchers. Hewit developed a good medical plan to support the Army. During battle, regimental surgeons were to remain with their regiments and provide immediate care after a soldier was wounded. Once the patient was stabilized, he walked or was moved by ambulance to a point a few hundred meters behind the lines where the ambulance train waited. From there, the wounded would move to a large hospital established by the Army. While Hewit had a good plan, the pace of the battle wrecked his efforts.

Most of the regimental surgeons lost all of their equipment when the Confederates overran the Union camps. On 6 April many Union surgeons remained with their wounded on the field and were captured. Many joint Union-Confederate hospitals were established on the battlefield. Surgeons established hospitals wherever they could find cover, including Grant's headquarters cabin at the landing, which was converted into a hospital. When the Army of the Ohio arrived to reinforce Grant, its surgeons were woefully unequipped. Surgeons had been ordered to leave their equipment behind, so they arrived on the battlefield with whatever they could carry.

On 7 April the first regular tent hospital ever was established on the Shiloh battlefield. Dr. B.J.D. Irwin, medical director, 4th Division, Army of the Ohio, established the hospital in COL David Stuart's camps on the eastern part of the battlefield. Irwin had many casualties and took possession of the abandoned tents and equipment in the area. Soon he had a well-organized, efficient field hospital. During the battle, the hospital ship *City of Memphis* and other boats from the Quartermaster Department evacuated wounded to Savannah where the entire town had been converted to a hospital. After the battle, the surgeons evacuated the wounded to the large hospitals farther north. The *City of Memphis* departed the landing on 8 April with 700 patients destined for Mound City.

The Quartermaster Department turned over steamers *Hiawatha*, *J.J. Roe*, *War Eagle*, and *Crescent City* to the medical department. A surgeon was placed on each steamer, and the boats were loaded with wounded bound for large general hospitals. Surgeons performed many operations on the voyages. Soon, civilian ships dispatched from the north arrived. The Sanitary Commission sent a boat loaded with badly needed supplies and evacuated patients on the return trip. Many state governors sent boats to evacuate wounded, but most would only carry wounded from their state, greatly adding to the confusion of this massive evacuation. A ship that the city of Louisville sent was the only civilian boat that would carry captured Confederate wounded. The Quartermaster Department sent additional ships to evacuate wounded, including the *Louisiana, D.A. January, Empress*, and *Imperial*.

The overworked Union surgeons did an adequate job with their limited supplies and experience. Although they had 8,400 Union and 1,000 Confederate casualties to care for, they established hospitals where they could and organized a system to quickly evacuate the wounded. While the excessive number of casualties overwhelmed them at Shiloh, they learned many lessons from this battle that they applied in future operations.

There is little specific information on Confederate medical support during the Battle of Shiloh. Generally, the Confederates had fewer surgeons and less supplies than the Union. Confederate hospitals sprang up in the captured Union camps. There, Confederate surgeons cared for the wounded, often using captured supplies. During the retreat on 7 April, the Confederates evacuated as many of their casualties as they could. Every wheeled vehicle was converted into an ambulance. Despite their best efforts, the Confederates left 1,000 of their wounded on the field. The Confederates established large hospitals in Corinth where civilian doctors and volunteers from all over the South converged to care for the wounded. Once the wounded were able to travel, trains evacuated them to hospitals in Jackson, Canton, Columbus, and Holly Springs.

Both sides cared for the enemy wounded as well as could be expected. Often on 6 April Union and Confederate surgeons worked side by side in Union camps. General Johnston's personal surgeon was not at Johnston's side when he was shot because he stopped to care for the wounded of both sides. After the battle, the Confederates returned seriously wounded prisoners to the Union because they could not care for them.

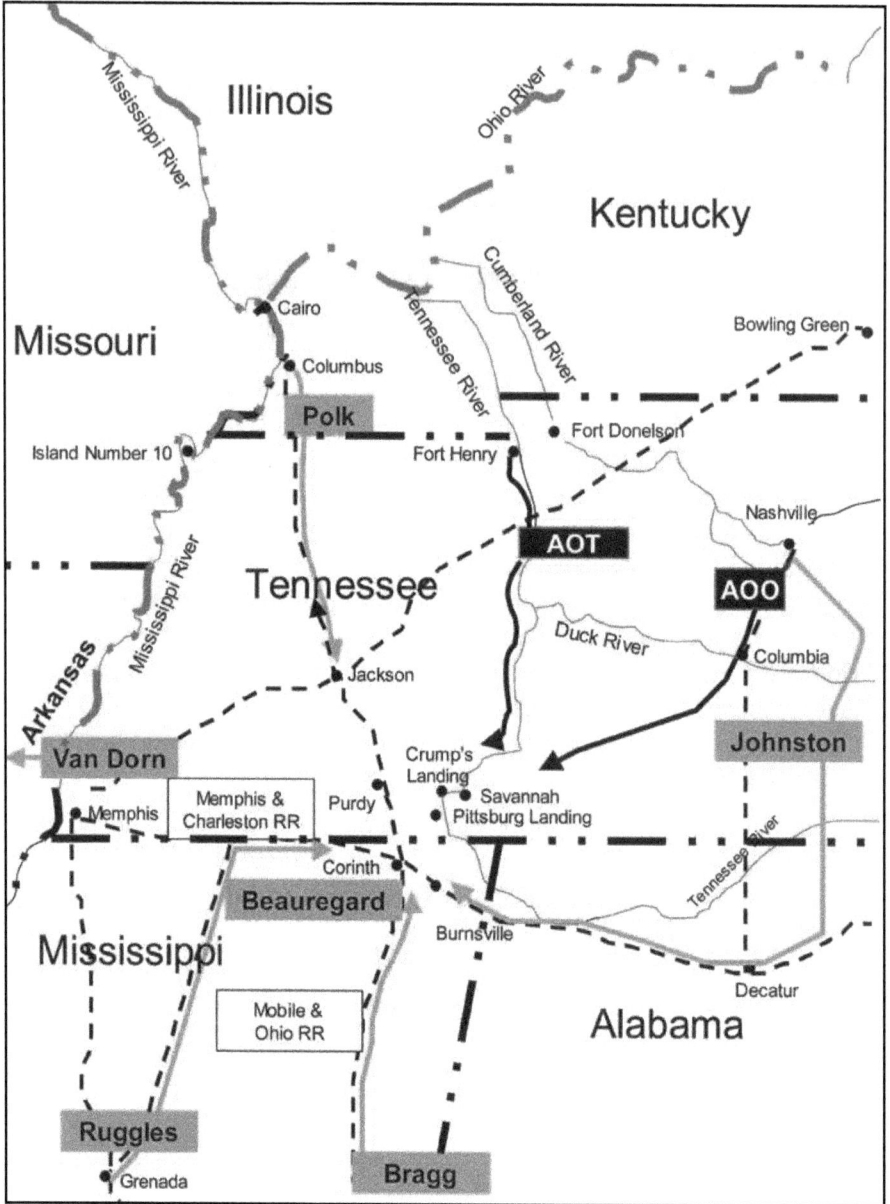

Map 1. Operational movement.

## II. Shiloh Campaign Overview

At the end of 1861 the Confederacy was still trying to maintain a cordon defense around all of the original territory of the southern states. The commander of all western Confederate troops was General Albert Sidney Johnston. To prevent a Union advance south into Tennessee or along the Mississippi River, Johnston had spread his forces in an irregular line that ran from Somerset, Kentucky, in the east to Columbus, Kentucky, in the west. By January 1862, the Confederate defensive line in the west was established.

MG George B. Crittenden had 6,000 troops spread between Somerset and Cumberland Gap, the natural route of advance to eastern Tennessee. At Bowling Green, a rail center with lines leading to Nashville and to Memphis, Johnston placed 23,000 troops under the command of MG William J. Hardee. At the western end of the line at Columbus, overlooking the Mississippi River, there were 12,000 troops under the command of MG Leonidas Polk. In between, Johnston defended his center with 5,000 troops in two forts along the Tennessee and Cumberland Rivers.

The Confederate Fort Henry protected the Tennessee River. Because of early political considerations, the fort was not located on the better terrain in Kentucky; rather, it was located in a very low place along the river in Tennessee. This poor location unfortunately meant that the fort was under water most of the time. Fort Donelson was located on commanding ground, and it protected the Cumberland River. Between these two forts the Confederates had 5,000 soldiers.

While the Confederates enjoyed a unified command in the west, the Union command was disjoined. MG Henry Halleck commanded the Department of Missouri, with headquarters in St. Louis. His area of responsibility began just east of the Cumberland River and ran to the west, including the Mississippi River. Halleck had 90,000 troops in his department. BG U.S. Grant had 20,000 troops along the Ohio and Mississippi Rivers in the vicinity of Cairo, Ilinois. BG John Pope had 15,000 troops in central Missouri. The remaining 55,000 troops were spread out west of Pope.

MG Don Carlos Buell commanded the Department of the Ohio with an area of responsibility comprised of the area east of Halleck's department to the Appalachian Mountains. Buell had 45,000 troops spread around central Kentucky. The first common link in the chain of command between Halleck and Buell was the War Department in Washington, a fact that hindered a united effort.

In December 1861 Halleck developed a strategic plan for piercing the Confederate cordon defense. Halleck determined that the ends of the Confederate defensive line were too strong to be taken easily but that piercing the line in the center would cause the entire Confederate line to collapse. Halleck determined that if he seized Forts Henry and Donelson, he would control the Cumberland and Tennessee Rivers, which would make the Confederate positions at Columbus and Bowling Green untenable.

On 19 January 1862 BG George Thomas, with 4,000 troops, attacked and defeated 4,000 troops under Crittenden at Mill Springs, Kentucky. The Confederate defeat opened an invasion route for the Union; only a few thousand Confederate troops blocked the Cumberland Gap. The defeat at Somerset helped the Confederate high command understand the size of Johnston's department, and they determined that he needed help. In response, Richmond sent General P.G.T. Beauregard to be Johnston's second in command. Beauregard had become a "thorn in the side" of the Confederate government. He and his troops had helped win the First Battle of Manassas, but now his forces had been combined with Johnston's forces, with Johnston commanding the combined force. Beauregard was now an "extra" general who voiced his unsolicited opinion to the government all the time. The territory in the east was much smaller than the west, so Richmond determined Beauregard would be of more use in the west. In January Beauregard was ordered to move to the west.

Halleck selected Grant to execute the reduction of the Confederate forts on the Tennessee and Cumberland Rivers, and Pope went to reduce the forts at Island Number 10 to open the Mississippi River to Memphis. Grant commanded the land forces while Commodore Andrew H. Foote led a flotilla of gunboats. The cooperating forces started operations from Cairo on 3 February. Unexpectedly, Fort Henry fell on 6 February after a short bombardment by Foote's gunboats. Almost immediately Grant moved his forces overland to Fort Donelson while Foote moved his flotilla up and over to the Cumberland River. While Grant moved, Johnston reinforced Fort Donelson to a strength of 21,000 troops, but he was too late. After an unsuccessful US naval attack and an equally unsuccessful Confederate breakout attempt, Grant seized Fort Donelson on 16 February. Grant captured 15,000 Confederate troops, but more importantly, the lower Tennessee and Cumberland Rivers were in Union hands. Federal gunboats could now traverse the entire length of the Tennessee River to Muscle Shoals, Alabama, and the Cumberland River was open to Nashville.

With the defeat at Mill Springs and the loss of Forts Henry and Donelson, the Confederate situation in the west was critical. Johnston's Confederate troops were now split; Johnston personally commanded 17,000 troops in the vicinity of Nashville facing Buell's 50,000 Union troops. Beauregard had 21,000 troops spread out from Columbus, Kentucky, to Corinth, Mississippi, facing 40,000 troops under Grant and 25,000 under Pope. The problem was that the Tennessee River split the Confederate troops. Confederate strategy was in a shambles. Something had to be done or all of Tennessee would be lost, and Mississippi and Alabama would be threatened.

Richmond authorities decided to reinforce Johnston's department. MG Braxton Bragg was ordered to reinforce middle Tennessee with 10,000 of his troops guarding the seacoast. BG Daniel Ruggles was ordered to come from Louisiana with 5,000 troops. Beauregard ordered Polk and his 17,000 troops to abandon Columbus and move to Corinth. Additionally, Johnston determined that he had to abandon the cordon defense and concentrate his troops. He selected Corinth as the point of concentration. Corinth was a critical rail hub where the east-west Memphis and Charleston Railroad crossed the north-south Mobile and Ohio Railroad. Johnston considered its defense to be critical for the Confederacy. Johnston ordered Beauregard to command the troops west of the Tennessee River while he moved his forces from Nashville. Johnston was taking a large gamble. 90,000 Union troops separated Johnston from Beauregard. Nashville was abandoned by 22 February, and with it tons of badly needed provisions and supplies were lost. Johnston moved to Murfreesboro, Tennessee, and on 28 February, he started his retreat south toward Corinth.

The Confederate populace and politicians were irritated by the defeats in the west, and all of them blamed Johnston. Luckily for Johnston, President Davis was behind him. When a delegation of Tennessee politicians asked him to replace Johnston, Davis said, "If Sydney Johnston is not a general, the Confederacy has none to give you." Johnston remained in command, but many had lost faith in him.

As Beauregard withdrew forces from Columbus, he left a large garrison at Island Number 10. Island Number 10 was the most northern Confederate defensive position on the Mississippi River. Beauregard determined that as long as Island Number 10 remained a threat Union forces under Pope could not campaign against Corinth. The Confederate fort at Island Number 10 had 8,000 troops and 51 cannon. Eventually, Beauregard reduced the island's garrison to 3,500 men and told the commander, BG William Mackall, that he had to fix Pope's troops. Mackall's 3,500 men tied down Pope's 25,000 men until Island Number 10 fell on 7 April. However, the defense of Island Number 10 tied down 25,000 Union soldiers during the Battle of Shiloh.

On 1 March gunboats *Tyler* and *Lexington* were traveling down the now-open Tennessee River when they discovered a battery of field artillery and a Confederate regiment at Pittsburg Landing. The gunboats opened fire and the Confederates soon retreated, having suffered a few casualties. The gunboats returned on 4 March and disembarked troops who moved inland 1 mile. The gunboat captains were convinced that the Confederates had permanently abandoned their defense of Pittsburg Landing, so they embarked the troops and moved on.

After the fall of Forts Henry and Donelson, Halleck decided to press his advantage. He moved Grant via the Tennessee River to seize Corinth and its vital rail lines. Once Corinth was secure, Halleck planned for Grant to seize Memphis. By seizing Memphis, Halleck believed that all of the Confederate forts on the Mississippi River north of Memphis would be untenable and either would be abandoned or easy prey to an invading force. To execute this plan, Halleck wanted Buell's troops. Halleck wanted to combine the two armies with him in command so their combined numbers could overwhelm the Confederates. He wanted Buell under his command, and he began pestering Washington for this new command.

The Union command arrangement was in turmoil as Halleck fought for his new organization. Halleck did not like Grant. Grant had gained a reputation for having a drinking problem while he was on active duty in the 1850s, and Halleck knew this. Grant had become a national hero after he took Fort Donelson, and Halleck now felt slighted. Additionally, Halleck and Buell did not like each other. Neither trusted the other, and they could not work together. Buell did not want to be under Halleck's command, and he would not cooperate with Halleck and his plans.

As Halleck continued to argue for overall command, he decided to start operations with or without Buell. He sent Buell numerous messages asking him to cooperate, but he decided to start movement without him. Halleck continued to increase the size of Grant's force. Grant had had four divisions for his campaign against the Confederate river forts, and as he started this new campaign, a new division under BG William T. Sherman was added to Grant's troop list. Surprisingly, as preparations for the campaign were under way, Halleck suddenly relieved Grant of command.

Halleck started out not liking Grant, and he found even more reasons to dislike him. Grant caught Halleck's ire after he crossed department lines by going to Nashville after he took Fort Donelson. Halleck was enraged that Grant had left the department's boundaries without permission (Grant had gone to coordinate with Buell). Halleck pestered Grant for reports on his strength and locations, and Grant's communication arrangements were poor. Grant was located at Fort Henry, and his messages went by boat to the telegraph station at Cairo where they were transmitted to Halleck in St. Louis. This situation was poor at best but was complicated because the telegraph operator at Cairo was a Confederate sympathizer who held some of Grant's messages. Halleck informed General in Chief George McClellan that he was having trouble with Grant and told him that Grant had "resumed his old habit," a reference to Grant's drinking. McClellan told Halleck to relieve Grant if it was for the best. On 4 March Halleck told Grant to remain at Fort Henry and turn command of the expedition over to MG Charles F. Smith, the senior division commander.

On 6 March the expedition, now under Smith, started south; by 9 March all of the troops were embarked and heading down the Tennessee River. Smith had 27,000 troops in five divisions with their full complement of cavalry and artillery. Smith's initial objective was Savannah, Tennessee, and his first troops arrived there on 8 March and started to disembark.

While Smith was moving, Halleck received good news. On 11 March Lincoln issued General Order #3. The order created the Department of the Mississippi by combining the Departments of the Ohio and Missouri. Halleck was placed in command of the new department. The Department of the Ohio became the Army of the Ohio, and Smith's troops became the Army of the Tennessee. Halleck now commanded Buell's troops, and on 16 March, Halleck ordered Buell to move his troops overland to the Tennessee River.

While the Union troops moved, Johnston kept moving to Corinth. After leaving Murfreesboro on 28 February, Johnston moved his forces to Fayetteville, Tennessee, arriving on 5 March. By 10 March, part of Johnston's troops arrived at Decatur, Alabama. Johnston planned to move his forces by rail from Decatur, but the Confederate rail system was in disarray. Still under civilian control, Bragg was using most of the railcars and engines to move his troops, so Johnston only had 160 cars to move his troops. Thus, the lack of railcars hindered Johnston's efforts to concentrate his forces. The first of Johnston's troops arrived in Corinth on 19 March, but troop units stretched all the way back to Decatur. Johnston himself finally arrived in Corinth on 22 March.

Having been told by Halleck to avoid battle until Buell arrived, Smith learned of the Confederate concentration at Corinth and decided to conduct two raids to cut vital rail links to Corinth. He sent one division under

MG Lew Wallace to Crump's Landing to cut the Mobile and Ohio rail lines at Bethel Station, Tennessee, and another division under Sherman to cut the same line east of Corinth at Burnsville, Mississippi. On 12 March, Smith went to see Wallace. While getting off of the boat, Smith badly scraped his leg from the knee to the ankle. The laceration seemed minor at first, but it would soon prove otherwise.

Wallace's division landed at Crump's Landing on 13 March. He sent his detachment of the 5th Ohio Cavalry to Bethel Station to damage the large rail trestle there. The cavalry was successful in damaging 150 feet of the trestle and returned to Crump's Landing. The Confederates sent a small force to Bethel Station to repair the line and to protect it.

On 14 March Sherman and his division loaded on transports and headed upriver toward Burnsville. As Sherman sailed past Pittsburg Landing, he became concerned that a Confederate force could occupy the bluffs and block his return route. He sent a message to Smith advising a division to move to and occupy Pittsburg Landing as a precaution. In response, Smith ordered BG Stephen A. Hurlbut's division to move to Pittsburg Landing.

Sherman arrived at Tyler's Landing on 14 March and quickly sent 400 troops of the 5th Ohio Cavalry to destroy a trestle in the vicinity Burnsville. The cavalry commander attempted the mission, but recent rainy weather had made crossing creeks and streams extremely treacherous. Finally the cavalry turned back when it could go no farther. Realizing the futility of continuing operations, Sherman embarked his command on the transports and sailed downstream. Sherman still wanted to accomplish the mission so he looked for the nearest accessible landing for a point to wait for better conditions. The Tennessee River was swollen, and the first place north of Tyler's Landing that Sherman could use was Pittsburg Landing.

Sherman ran into Hurlbut's troops at Pittsburg Landing. Leaving both divisions embarked at the landing, Sherman continued to Savannah to discuss the matter with Smith. Sherman suggested to Smith that he should occupy Pittsburg Landing and attempt an advance on the railroads from there. Sherman was convincing, and Smith ordered him to occupy Pittsburg Landing with his own division and Hurlbut's.

Sherman returned to Pittsburg Landing and conducted a personal reconnaissance before landing the troops. Convinced that there were no Confederate troops nearby, he disembarked the troops. Early the next morning Sherman sent his cavalry toward Corinth to destroy the Mobile and Ohio line. Soon the cavalry returned, reporting that they had encountered Confederate cavalry. Sherman was now convinced that he could not cut the railroad, so he ordered his troops to bivouac about ¾ of a mile from the landing.

On 15 March Grant resumed command of the Army of the Tennessee. President Lincoln had found out about his dismissal and told Halleck to provide specific information on Grant. Halleck backed down. He informed the War Department that he was satisfied with Grant's explanation and would return him to command. On 16 March, Grant departed Fort Henry and arrived on the 17th at Savannah, where he established his headquarters.

When Grant arrived at Savannah, he found Smith confined to a bed because his abrasion had developed a tetanus infection. Grant had two divisions at Pittsburg Landing and one at Crump's Landing with the rest of the army at Savannah. Based on Sherman's report, Grant ordered the troops at Savannah, except for McClernand's division, to move to Pittsburg Landing and go into camp. Grant wanted McClernand to remain in Savannah because he outranked Sherman; Grant wanted Sherman to be the senior commander at Pittsburg Landing.

Despite having most of his troops at Pittsburg Landing, Grant kept his headquarters at Savannah. With Smith ill and McClernand at Savannah, Sherman was in charge at Pittsburg Landing. Sherman placed most of his division in camps blocking the Corinth Road. He placed Stuart's brigade of his division in camps astride the Hamburg-Savannah Road, the only other avenue of approach to Pittsburg Landing. As other divisions arrived, Sherman assigned them camps. Hurlbut's division went into camps southwest of the landing along the Hamburg-Savannah Road. Smith's division, temporarily under W.H.L. Wallace's command, occupied camps along the Pittsburg Landing Road.

Sherman had given detailed instructions for establishing camps. He wanted camps tactically situated where the men could occupy battle lines quickly. However, most commanders established their camps based on comfort, not tactical dispositions. Camps were located based on water supplies and good camping grounds. Additionally, Sherman did not believe it was necessary to prepare fortifications because he was convinced the Confederates were at Corinth with no intent to move, and building fortifications would demoralize the Union men.

As soon as the Union troops had established their camps, commanders began a regimen of drills and reviews. The area around Pittsburg Landing was heavily wooded, with occasional open fields. Union commanders used these open areas as drill fields and review fields. Many of the troops were new to the Army and badly needed the training.

On the Confederate side, the last of Johnston's troops arrived at Corinth on 27 March; 49,000 troops were now concentrated around Corinth. In consultation with his commanders, Johnston decided he would attack Grant's army before it combined with Buell's. He also decided that with the influx of troops his army had to be reorganized. The mission fell to Beauregard. Beauregard named the army the Army of the Mississippi and reorganized it. He created four corps within the army. MG Polk would command the I Corps, a two-division corps with 9,000 men. MG Bragg would command the 13,000-man, two-division II Corps. MG Hardee would command the III Corps. This corps would only have three brigades with no division structure. Finally, Beauregard created a Reserve Corps and gave BG John C. Breckinridge command. Like the III Corps, the Reserve Corps would have three brigades with no division structure. Bragg was named the Army Chief of Staff in addition to being a corps commander.

Grant finally decided to send all of his troops to Pittsburg Landing. McClernand's division moved from Savannah on 20 March and occupied camps to the rear of Sherman's camps. By 22 March Grant realized that Smith could not take the field, so he made W.H.L. Wallace the commander of Smith's division. On 26 March Grant created a 6th Division from newly arriving units with BG Benjamin Prentiss as its commander. Prentiss went into camp between Sherman's division and Stuart's brigade. Sherman and Prentiss had the "greenest" troops in the Army, and their divisions now occupied the exterior lines of the Army's encampment.

While Grant established his camp and Johnston reorganized, Buell continued to move. He left Nashville on 16 March, and by 19 March his troops were at the Duck River, about 80 miles from Savannah. The Confederates had destroyed all of the bridges over the river, so Buell stopped. For seven days Buell's troops tried to bridge the river. Finally, BG William Nelson convinced Buell to try to ford the river. For the next three days, the Army of the Ohio forded the Duck River, but the destroyed bridges had stopped Buell for 10 days. Once across the river, Buell continued marching toward the Tennessee River.

While Sherman was in camp, his troops had sporadic contact with Confederate cavalry. On 24 March Sherman led two of his brigades on a reconnaissance south of his camps toward Corinth. Sherman did not make contact, but the Confederates had seen his movement and were concerned about Union aggressiveness.

All of the Army of the Tennessee was now in the vicinity of Pittsburg Landing except MG Lew Wallace's division, which remained encamped in the vicinity of Crump's Landing. Wallace was concerned that he was more than 4 miles from the concentrated Army, so he decided to prepare a route to the Army. He had two options. The River Road closely paralleled the Tennessee River, and it ended at BG W.H.L. Wallace's camps along the Pittsburg Landing Road. The Shunpike Road twisted through the countryside and ended at Sherman's camps. Both roads were in appalling condition.

After a personal reconnaissance, Lew Wallace decided to repair the Shunpike as his route to the Army. He considered it the better of the two roads and felt it would be easier to repair. On 31 March Confederates from Purdy harassed the Union troops working on the road. Wallace was concerned and deployed his entire division toward the threat. The Confederates saw this and retreated to Purdy. When this action was reported to Johnston, he was concerned that the move meant an impending attack by the entire Army of the Tennessee. He sent MG Benjamin Franklin Cheatham's division to Purdy to stabilize the situation, but he determined that the Army of the Ohio had to be near. At that moment Johnston decided he had to attack Grant immediately, before the Army of the Ohio joined him.

On 2 April Johnston went to see Bragg. Beauregard had sent Johnston a telegram telling him the time was right to attack. Johnston laid out the information about MG Lew Wallace's division and that he had learned Buell had crossed the Duck River and was again moving. Bragg agreed with Beauregard's assessment. Johnston told an aide to write a dispatch to the corps commanders telling them to be prepared to advance the next morning.

The Confederate plan called for a departure at 0600 on 3 April. Hardee's corps was to lead on the Ridge Road, followed by Clark's division of Polk's corps. Polk would consolidate his corps when Cheatham came down from Purdy and linked up. Bragg would travel along the Monterey Road followed by Breckinridge. Once the Army reached a small farmhouse named Michie's, it would form for the attack. Johnston planned to attack with his four corps in successive lines. Hardee's corps would lead, followed in sequence by Bragg, Polk, and Breckinridge. The main goal of Johnston's attack was to turn Grant's left, driving the Federals away from the Tennessee River. Johnston and Beauregard used this particular attack formation because they were short of experienced officers and because the terrain was difficult.

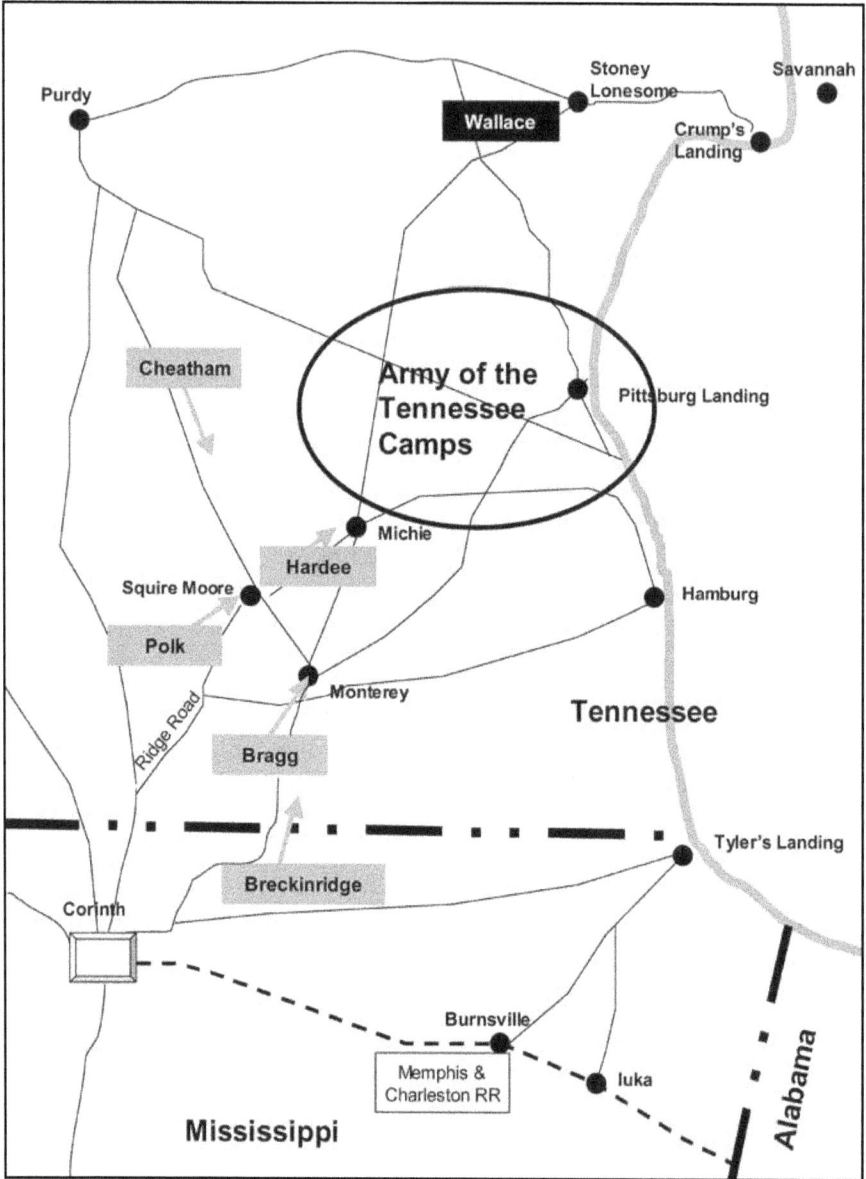

Map 2.

The Confederate movement was a debacle from the start. The streets of Corinth were so clogged that the start time was pushed back. Commanders battled among themselves for road use, which caused confusion and delay. Bragg's troops got a late start due to an error in their orders. Cheatham's division never started this day because of vague orders. Hardee's troops turned off the main road to find a bivouac location, but Polk's troops continued on the main road. It rained the night of 3 April, and the Confederates slept in the open.

On the morning of 4 April the disjointed advance continued. When Hardee's troops returned to the main road, they found Polk in the way. Much time was lost as Hardee attempted to pass Polk. The Confederates made poor time, and a rainstorm in the afternoon again slowed the advance. By the night of 4 April the Army of the Mississippi was widely dispersed between Corinth and Michie's farmhouse. Johnston met with Beauregard, Bragg, and Breckinridge on the night of the 4th. Johnston ordered an attack on Grant's troops for the next morning at 0800.

During the night the rain came in torrents, soaking the Confederates lying in the open fields. As the corps commanders attempted to move their troops to their starting positions, the rain and darkness caused them to halt movement. The Confederates did not start their movement on 5 April until 0700. At 1000 Hardee's troops began to deploy into the line of battle and soon were ready to attack. Bragg was to form the next line behind Hardee, but his troops were delayed and not in position until 1600. Once Bragg was in line, Polk quickly moved into position. Cheatham's division had moved that morning and linked up with his corps. By the time the fourth line, Breckinridge's corps, was in position, it was dark.

The Union troops were not completely unaware of the Confederates' presence. On 4 April an advance picket from the 77th Ohio Regiment of Sherman's division saw a large number of Confederates around Seay Field. They reported their sighting, but Sherman dismissed it. Later that day, one of the picket posts of the 72d Ohio Regiment of Sherman's division was captured. After the capture, Sherman sent his cavalry to investigate. The cavalry ran into a long line of infantry and some artillery. COL Ralph Buckland, one of Sherman's brigade commanders, brought up some infantry to support the cavalry. After a brief skirmish, the Union forces withdrew to their lines. When Buckland reported what he saw, Sherman replied, "You militia officers get scared too easily."

Grant came to Pittsburg Landing when he learned of the firing, arriving after dark. As he made his way to Sherman's camp in the dark and rain, his horse fell, pinning his leg between the saddle and the ground and severely spraining his ankle. Grant would be on crutches for the next few days, thus reducing his mobility and capacity to move around the battlefield.

The indications of a Confederate presence continued on 5 April. COL Jesse Appler, commander, 53d Ohio Regiment, was concerned and sent

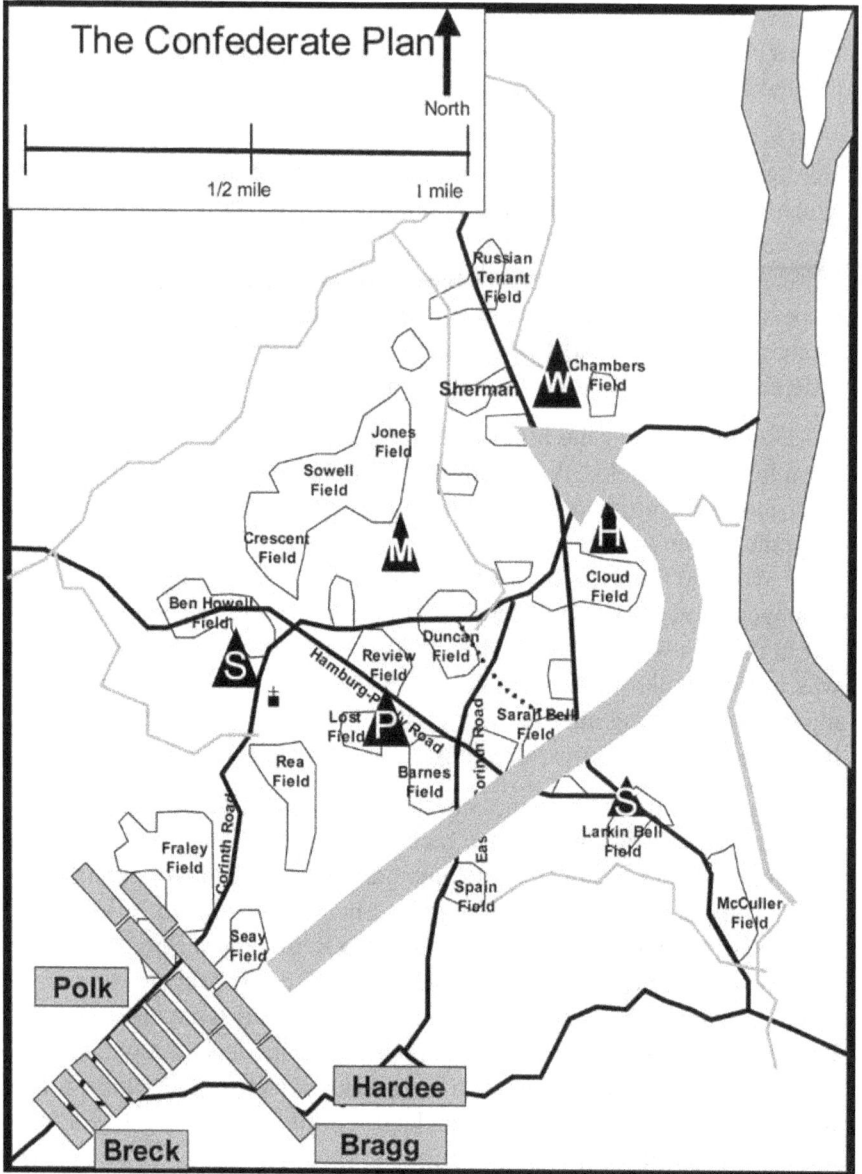

Map 3.

out a reconnaissance party. The party soon made contact, and Appler formed his regiment and sent an officer to report to Sherman. The officer soon returned with Sherman's reply, "Take your damn regiment to Ohio. There is no enemy nearer than Corinth!" On the afternoon of the 5th, BG Prentiss reviewed his entire division in Spain Field. Major James Powell of the 25th Missouri noticed Confederates watching the review and received permission to conduct a reconnaissance. Powell's patrol did not make contact but did hear noise indicating a large Confederate presence. Powell reported this information to his brigade commander, COL Everett Peabody.

5 April was a day of reorganization in the Army of the Tennessee. Grant had decided to reorganize his army's cavalry and artillery. The reorganization occurred on 5 April. Sherman lost his detachment of the 5th Ohio Cavalry Regiment and received a detachment from the 4th Illinois Cavalry Regiment. During the daylight hours of 5 April Sherman had no cavalry because of the reorganization.

On the evening of 5 April the Confederate commanders met. Once Bragg's troops were in position, Beauregard rode up and conferred with Bragg. Both generals agreed that the Union had to know of the Confederates' presence and had to be entrenched. They thought it best to fall back to Corinth without a fight. They sent for Polk, and while Beauregard, Bragg, and Polk talked, Johnston rode up. It was 1700. Beauregard and Bragg recommended to Johnston that the Army retreat to Corinth. The reasons they stated were that they would have had to have lost surprise, the Union troops had to be entrenched, and the soldiers had eaten all of their rations. Johnston asked Polk for his opinion, and Polk recommended they attack. Breckinridge rode up and stated his corps was ready to attack. Johnston looked at the assembled generals and said, "Gentlemen, we shall attack at daylight tomorrow." The corps commanders returned to their troops. As Johnston was leaving the meeting, he turned to an aide and said, "I would fight them if they were a million."

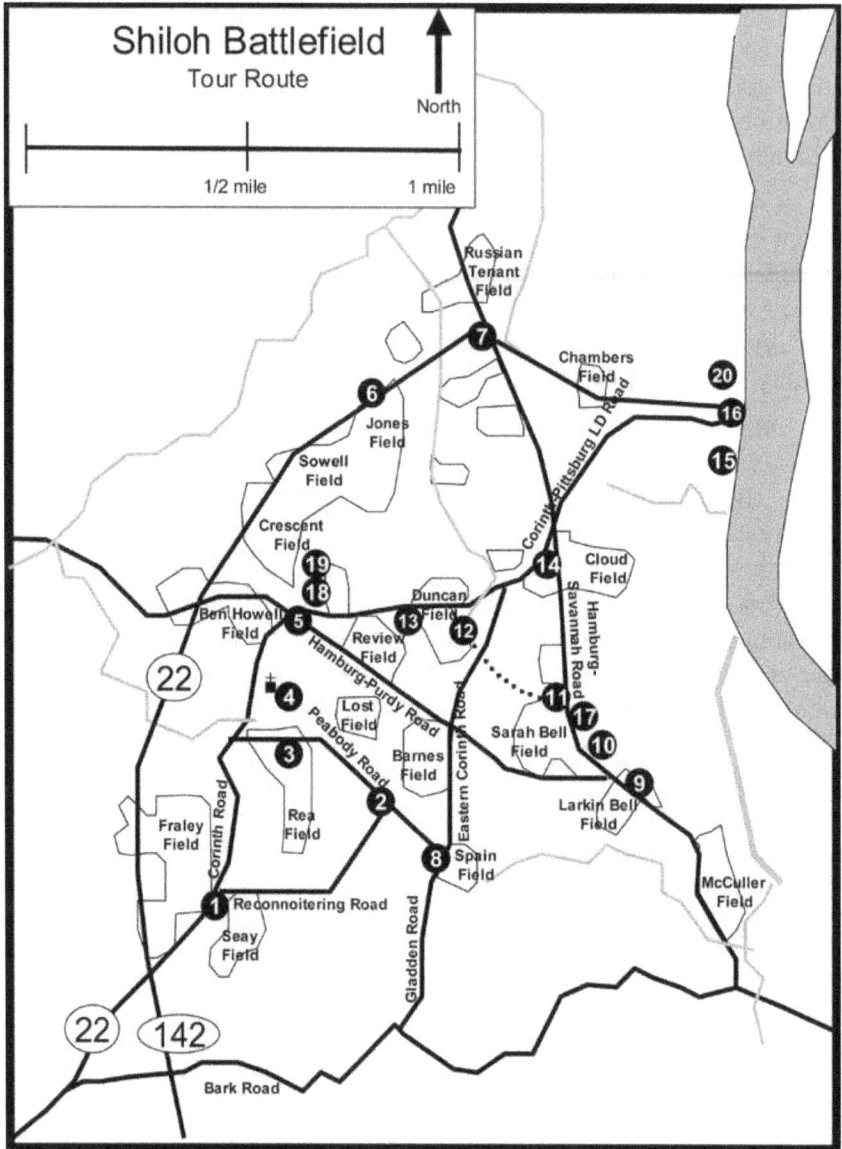

Map 4.

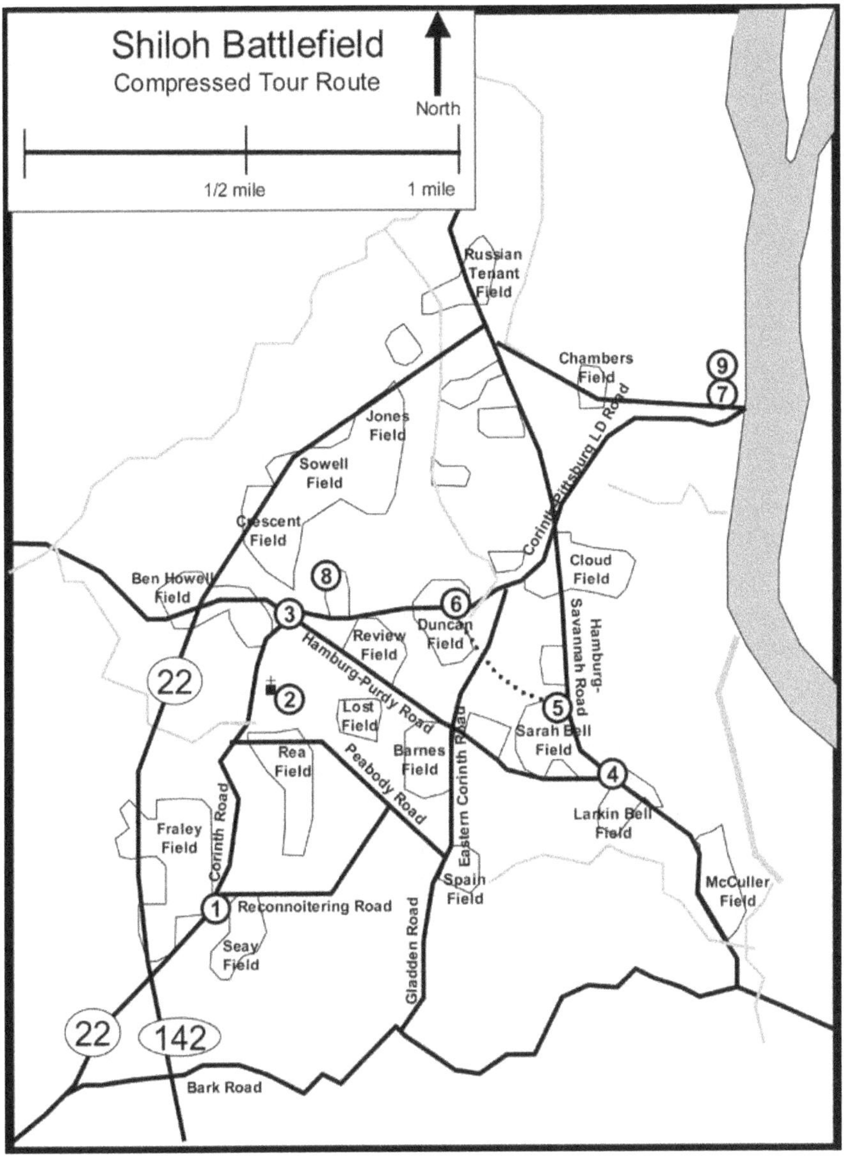

Shiloh Battlefield
Compressed Tour Route
North
1/2 mile
1 mile
Russian Tenant Field
Chambers Field
Jones Field
Sowell Field
Crescent Field
Corinth-Pittsburg LD Road
Cloud Field
Ben Howell Field
Review Field
Duncan Field
Hamburg-Purdy Road
Hamburg-Savannah Road
22
Lost Field
Rea Field
Barnes Field
Sarah Bell Field
Peabody Road
Eastern Corinth Road
Corinth Road
Fraley Field
Larkin Bell Field
McCuller Field
Spain Field
Reconnoitering Road
Gladden Road
Seay Field
22
142
Bark Road


Map 5.

# III. Suggested Routes and Vignettes

## Introduction

The Battle of Shiloh occurred over a two-day period in a large area of rugged, wooded terrain. This guide is designed to examine the entire battle during a one-day visit. To accomplish this, a very early start is required. Groups should carefully examine this guide and plan their visit, adjusting stand times as required. Most of this guide requires driving between stands, although there are a few places where one may leave a vehicle and complete a couple of stands before returning to it.

Due to the terrain and road conditions, this guide examines the battle in sectors rather than sequentially in time. First we examine the attacks on the Confederate left/Union right. Then we transition to the fight on the Confederate right/Union left. The recommended route follows no signs or monuments. Directions are as specific as possible, but group leaders should use the vehicle odometer to track distances. Directions for the route are sometimes given in cardinal directions rather than "left or right." Group leaders should have a compass.

Before starting, the group leader should check in with the park headquarters to obtain information on road conditions and other park conditions. He may want to begin the staff ride at a location where he can discuss the strategic and operational overview (part II of this guide). Locations for this stand could be Pittsburg Landing by the park headquarters or at Wood's Field in the southwest portion of the park.

If time is critical during the staff ride, use the route on map 5, "Shiloh Battlefield Compressed Tour Route." This route will take approximately 4 to 5 hours versus 7 to 8 hours for the "full" route. You can conduct the following stands from each stop (a white circle with a black number marks stops on the map):

Stop 1: Stands 1, 2

Stop 2: Stands 3, 4

Stop 3: Stands 5, 6, and 7

Stop 4: Stands 8, 9, and 10

Stop 5: Stand 11

Stop 6: Stands 12, 13, and 14

Stop 7: Stands 15, 16

Stop 8: Stands 17, 18, and 19

Stop 9: Stand 20

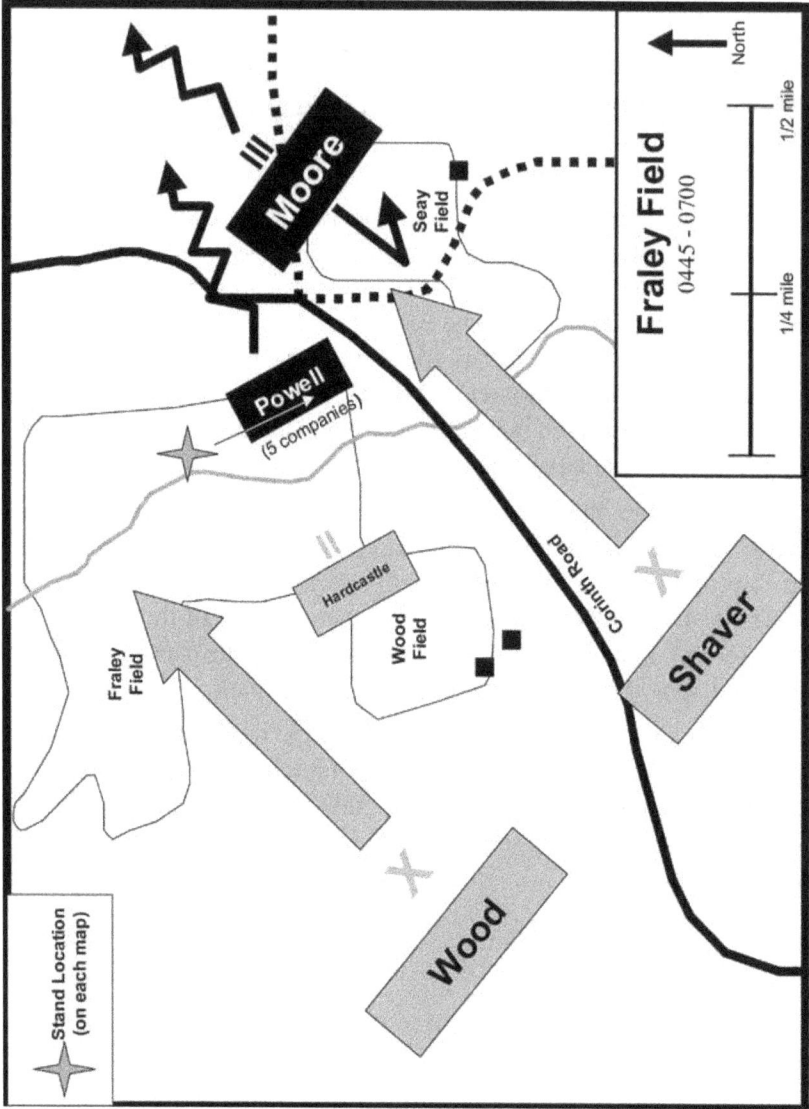

# Fraley Field
## 0445 - 0700

North

1/4 mile  1/2 mile

Moore

III

Seay Field

Powell
(5 companies)

Hardcastle

Wood Field

Fraley Field

Corinth Road

Shaver

X

X

Wood

Stand Location
(on each map)

Map 6.

# Stand 1

## Fraley Field

*Directions:* Starting at the park headquarters, travel west 1.1 miles on Pittsburg Landing Road. Turn left (south) on TN 22 and travel 1.7 miles. Turn left (east) on Hamburg-Purdy Road and travel .4 mile. Turn right (south) on Corinth Road and travel 1.2 miles (bear to the right at the "Y" intersection). As the road ends and turns to the left (east), park the vehicle. Take the trail to the west (there are two metal tablets and an open field visible from the vehicle). Go 50 meters into the field; you are now in Fraley Field.

*Description:* COL Everett Peabody, commander, 1st Brigade, 6th Division (Prentiss) was worried about reports of a Confederate presence. Early on the evening of 5 April he debriefed a patrol from the 25th Missouri. The patrol's leader, Major James Powell, reported that he heard a large body of Confederates south of the camps. Very early on 6 April Peabody, on his own authority, ordered Powell to conduct another reconnaissance with three companies from the 25th Missouri and two companies of the 12th Michigan. At 0300 Powell formed five companies and cautiously headed south.

During the night the Confederates had slept on their arms. BG S.A.M. Wood's brigade of Hardee's corps was in the front line, and before darkness, Wood had placed Major A.B. Hardcastle's 3d Mississippi Battalion in front of his brigade as skirmishers.

At approximately 0445 Powell's skirmish line entered Fraley Field. When it was partially across, Hardcastle's troops opened fire. Powell's men took cover on the east side of the field, and for the next 60 minutes these small units traded fire, causing minor casualties. During the fight Prentiss learned that his troops were in contact so he ordered COL David Moore to take five of his companies of the 21st Missouri (Peabody's brigade) to assist Powell.

At 0630 Powell noticed some Confederate cavalry moving to his left. Fearing he was being flanked, Powell ordered his men to withdraw. As Powell withdrew, the general Confederate advance began. Continuing his withdrawal, Powell met Moore coming up with the relief column. Moore, after berating Powell for retreating, took charge of the troops now in Seay Field. The rest of the 21st Missouri soon joined Moore along the eastern edge of Seay Field. Moore led these troops across the field, and when he was halfway across, the Confederates hidden along the west side of the field opened fire. Moore was wounded in the leg and soon ordered a retreat to the northeast corner of the field.

Confederate COL R.G. Shaver was also in the front line of Hardee's corps, to the right of Wood. When the order to advance was given, his brigade entered Seay Field from the southwest and exchanged fire with the 21st Missouri. After some delay, Shaver advanced across the field and sent the 21st Missouri retreating back to its camps. Shaver and the rest of the Confederates continued their attack.

*Vignette 1:* Henry Stanley was a private in the 6th Arkansas of Shaver's brigade. Later he would become a journalist and earn unending fame for his search in Africa for Dr. David Livingstone, "Dr. Livingstone I presume." Stanley reflected on the opening of the battle:

"We loaded our muskets and arranged our cartridge pouches ready for use. Our weapons were the obsolete flintlocks, and the ammunition was rolled in cartridge-paper, which contained powder, a round ball, and three buckshot. . . . Within a few minutes, there was another explosive burst of musketry, the air was pierced by many missiles, which hummed and pinged sharply by our ears, pattered throughout the tree-tops, and brought twigs and leaves down on us. 'Those are bullets' Henry whispered in awe. . . . 'There they are!' was no sooner uttered, than we cracked into them with levelled (sic) muskets. 'Aim low men!' commanded Captain Smith. I tried hard to see some living thing to shoot at, for it appeared absurd to be blazing away at the shadows. . . . My nerves tingled, my pulse beat double quick, my heart throbbed loudly, almost painfully. . . . I was angry with my rear rank because he made my eyes smart with the powder of his musket; and I felt like cuffing him for deafening my ears!" (Private Henry Stanley, 6th Arkansas, quoted in Henry M. Stanley, *The Autobiography of Sir Henry Morton Stanley*, Cambridge, MA: Riverside Press, 1909, 187-90.)

*Vignette 2:* As General Albert Sidney Johnston ordered the attack to commence, he turned to his aides: "Tonight, we will water our horses in the Tennessee River." (William P. Johnston, *The Life of General Albert Sidney Johnston*, New York: 1878.)

*Teaching point 1:* Reconnaissance. Was the cavalry optimally organized for each side, and what was its mission? What did each side know about the enemy, and could/should they have known more?

*Teaching point 2:* Initiative. Was Peabody correct to send out a patrol when he was told not to bring on an engagement?

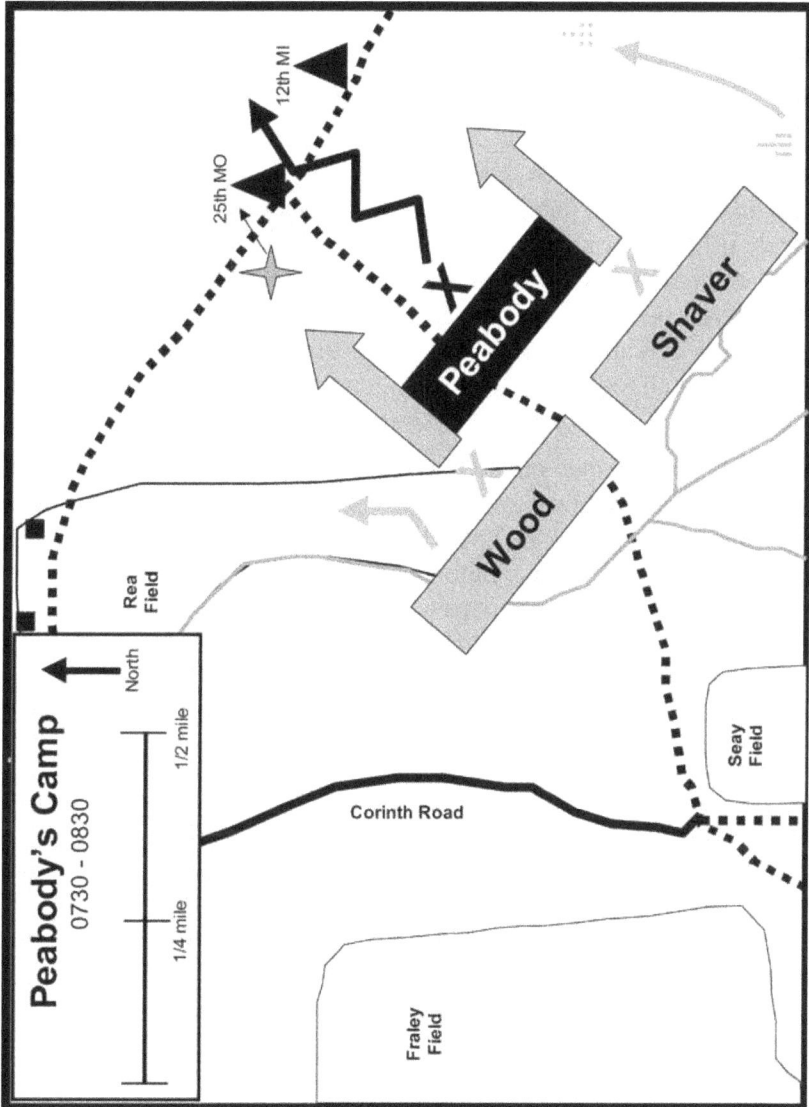

Peabody's Camp
0730 - 0830

North

1/4 mile    1/2 mile

Fraley Field

Corinth Road

Seay Field

Rea Field

Wood

Shaver

Peabody

25th MO

12th MI

Map 7.

63

# Stand 2

## Peabody's Camps

*Directions:* Travel east on Reconnoitering Road for .7 mile. As you are driving, notice the slight ridge with the tablets; this is where COL Peabody initially formed his brigade. At the intersection, pull into the parking spot straight ahead. Dismount the vehicle and walk to Peabody's death marker. You are now in the location of Peabody's brigade camps.

*Description:* Peabody had sent almost half of his brigade forward to Seay Field. As he received reports of its actions, he ordered the remaining two regiments into the line of battle. Soon BG Prentiss rode up and asked Peabody if he had brought on this battle. Peabody replied that he had ordered a reconnaissance. Prentiss was angered and said, "COL Peabody, I will hold you personally responsible for bringing on this engagement." Peabody was now angered and told Prentiss that he was responsible for all of his actions and rode off to form his troops. He occupied a position on a slight ridge south of his camps. The time was 0730.

Soon Peabody's men on the line were greeted with a curious sight— dozens of rabbits running toward them. Soon Powell's reconnaissance party returned and joined the line, closely followed by the 21st Missouri, which also went into the line. Before long Confederates appeared, marching toward their lines. These troops were Shaver's men and part of Wood's brigade; two regiments had split and were heading north toward Rhea Field. When Shaver's men were 75 yards distant, Peabody opened fire. Shaver was stopped and one of his regiments broke. The two sides traded shots at this close range, but no one advanced.

Soon Swett's Confederate battery occupied a position to the right of Shaver. While their fire was effective, Swett was in danger of becoming ineffective because so many of his men were being shot. To relieve the battery, Hardee ordered Shaver and Wood to charge. Peabody's troops could not stand the assault and soon retreated. Peabody, who had been wounded four times already, attempted to rally his troops. While mounted on his horse, he was shot in the head and killed. By 0900 the combination of the Confederate attack and the death of their commander was more than the Federal troops could handle. They broke for the rear. The Confederates had captured their first Union camp.

*Vignette:* One of the soldiers assigned to Peabody's brigade describes the night before battle: "All day Saturday we had the instinctive feeling that a great battle was imminent. . . . We felt that we were going to be arrayed in a deadly conflict and that some of us would probably pay the price of loyalty and be numbered with the slain. On Saturday evening a number of us gathered in one of the large Silbey Tents we were then using. One of the boys struck up a song in which we all joined. The song was followed by others, and the spell, which seemed to be over all caused us with one accord, to sing the songs of home and bygone days. Our last song was 'Brave Boys are They.' How the words come back to me today!

> 'Thinking no less of them,
> Loving our country the more.
> We sent them forth to fight for the flag
> Their fathers before them bore.'

We closed the evening's singing with these lines:

> 'Oh! The dread field of battle!
> Soon to be strewn with graves!
> If brothers fall, then bury them where
> Our banner in triumph waves.'

The singing ended, and under the spell of its patriotic pathos, without uttering a word, we separated and each man retired to his own tent; some to dream of homes to which they would never return, and of friends they would never meet this side of the 'eternal shore.' That little company never met again." (Private Jacob Fawcett, 16th Wisconsin Infantry, Jacob Fawcett, "Address at the Dedication of the Monument Erected by the State of Wisconsin on the Battlefield of Shiloh in Memory of Her Soldiers Who Fought on the Field" published in *Wisconsin at Shiloh*, compiled by F.H. Magdeburg, Madison, WI: Wisconsin Shiloh Monument Commission, 1909, 89.)

*Teaching point 1:* Battle command. Was Peabody successfully commanding his brigade? Was Prentiss a help or a hindrance?

*Teaching point 2:* Preparedness. Were the Union camps tactically laid out and mutually supporting? How could Prentiss have better laid out his camps so the men were comfortable but ready for battle?

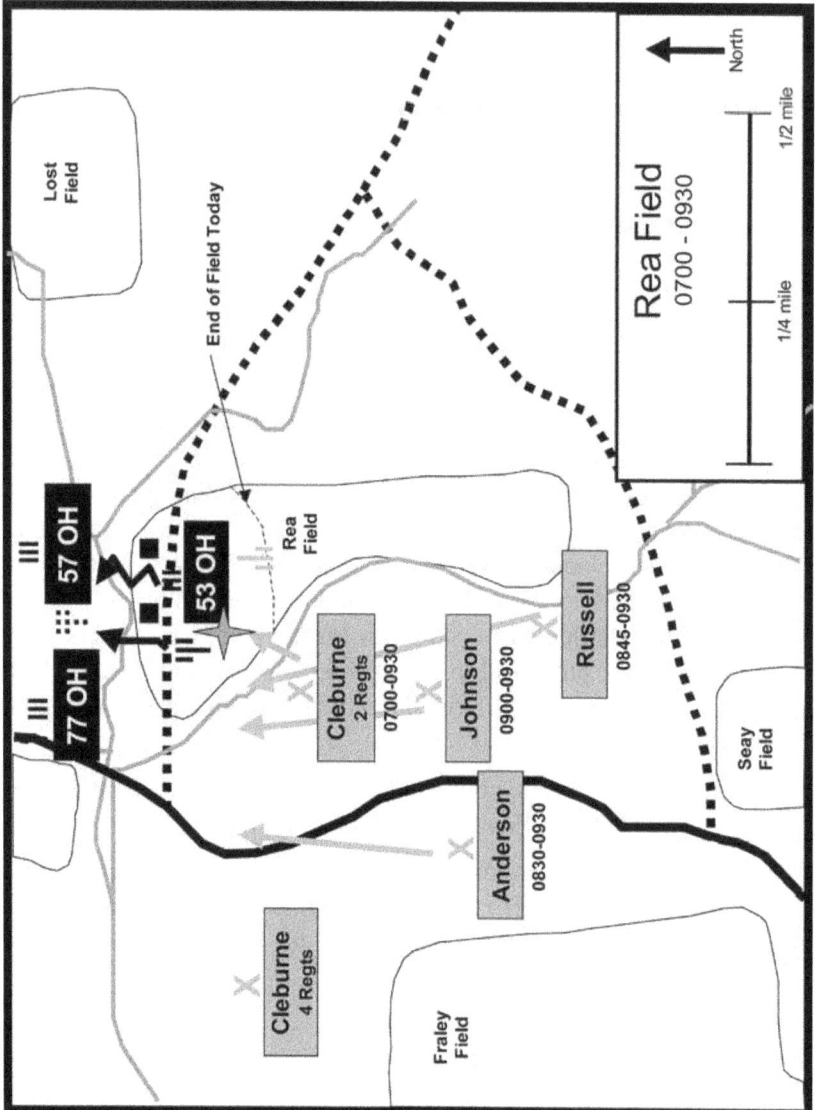

Rea Field
0700 - 0930

North

1/4 mile    1/2 mile

Map 8.

Lost Field

End of Field Today

57 OH

53 OH

Rea Field

77 OH

Cleburne
2 Regts
0700-0930

Johnson
0900-0930

Russell
0845-0930

Anderson
0830-0930

Cleburne
4 Regts

Fraley Field

Seay Field

66

# Stand 3

## Rea Field

*Directions:* Travel northwest on Peabody Road for .7 mile. Pull off the road opposite the two cannons in the field on your left (south). Dismount the vehicle and walk south to the 53d Ohio's marker. You are in Rea Field.

*Description:* COL Jesse Hildebrand's brigade of Sherman's division was in camps around Rea Field. The 53d Ohio Regiment had its camp in Rea Field. COL Jesse Appler, commander, 53d Ohio had heard the firing to his south early in the morning. He wanted to put his troops on the line, but the rebuke from Sherman the previous day was still fresh in his head. When a wounded soldier came retreating through the camp yelling for the men to get on the line, Appler formed his regiment. Appler sent an aide to tell Hildebrand and Sherman. The aide that went to Sherman returned and told Appler "General Sherman says you must be badly scared over there."

Confederate BG Patrick Cleburne commanded a brigade in Hardee's corps. He was in line to the left of Wood. As his troops approached Rea Field, they split. Three of his regiments remained west of the stream running to the west of the field while the remaining two, with Cleburne, crossed the stream and entered Rea Field.

Captain A.C. Waterhouse deployed his Illinois battery to support the 53d Ohio. At 0700 Sherman and an orderly rode to Appler's line to investigate. As Sherman was examining the terrain, Cleburne attacked. A soldier told Sherman, "Look to your right." Sherman was finally convinced as he uttered, "My God, we are attacked." Cleburne's troops fired and Sherman's orderly was killed; Sherman was shot in the hand with a buckshot from a "buck and ball" cartridge. Sherman rode to Appler and told him to hold on while he promised to get him some support. Appler, assisted by Waterhouse's battery, repulsed three charges by Cleburne's troops. One of Cleburne's regiments, the 6th Mississippi, suffered more than 70-percent casualties in Rea Field.

Sherman rode to Hildebrand and told him to deploy his remaining two regiments. The 57th and 77th Ohio formed but remained north of the field. Appler's troops had been fighting well, but Appler suddenly lost his composure and yelled, "Retreat and save yourselves!" The 53d Ohio abandoned its position in the Rea Field and retreated to the vicinity of Lost Field. Waterhouse's battery withdrew to Shiloh Church.

At 0830 BG Patton Anderson's brigade from Bragg's second line came up to support Cleburne. Anderson attacked up Corinth Road but was repulsed by Buckland's brigade and Waterhouse's battery. At 0845 COL Robert M. Russell's brigade from Polk's corps attacked through Rea Field, but it too was repulsed. At 0900 Polk's Confederate battery went into position in Rea Field and dueled with Waterhouse. As soon as Polk's battery was in position, BG Bushrod Johnson's brigade from Polk's corps unsuccessfully attacked. For 2 hours Buckland's and Hildebrand's brigades and one battery had held up four Confederate brigades that had attacked seven times using piecemeal frontal attacks.

At 0930 the Confederates were finally able to coordinate their attack. Anderson, Russell, and Cleburne attacked simultaneously. The remnants of Hildebrand's brigade and Waterhouse's battery retreated toward Shiloh Church.

*Vignette:* A lieutenant in Cleburne's brigade described his first combat: "Presently, I began to see men on the ground and soon realized they were hurt. At first I couldn't see their faces. Maybe I didn't want to see them. The first wounded man I recognized was my Uncle Henry's eldest son, cousin James Mangum, a private in my company. He had been shot in the face. I wanted to stop and help him, but everyone was moving forward, all seemed to be hollering at the top of their lungs. We just had to get to those Federals who were shooting us; therefore there was no time to help the wounded. I did manage to tell James, as I stopped briefly beside him, to take shelter behind a large oak. Most of the men on the ground were our close friends, neighbors, kinfolk. I saw Stephen Gordon but knew I could not help him. His eyes were glazing over. He was dead. Next I came to Elias McLendon. He was badly wounded. It was awful, but I keep on moving. I had not gone far when a sudden pain hit me. My legs folded and I was on the ground. I had been yelling, but the fall knocked the breath out of me, and I was quiet. . . . I must have fainted, for the next thing I knew someone had me by the shoulders and was dragging me out of the line of fire. He helped me to get to the hospital area. I didn't recognize who had helped me until I had gone some distance. He was our major, Pat Brandon, who was also wounded." (Lieutenant William Thompson, 6th Mississippi, in William C. Thompson, "From Shiloh to Port Gibson," *Civil War Times Illustrated*, October 1964, 20.)

*Teaching point 1:* Synchronization. Why were the initial Confederate attacks in Rea Field not synchronized? Who was responsible for synchronizing them?

*Teaching point 2:* Mass. How did Hildebrand's brigade hold off four Confederate brigades for so long? What was the effect when the Confederates finally massed troops in Rea Field?

*Teaching point 3:* Fire support. Who directed Waterhouse's battery? Was Waterhouse's fire important to this fight?

***Side Trip:*** Confederate Burial Trench. (You should only do this side trip if you decide to use the compressed route because you will conduct a stand at another Confederate burial trench on the full route.) Continue 75 yards to the south and you will be at one of the five known Confederate burial trenches. After the battle, Union troops quickly buried the dead of both sides. They took care to bury their own dead who were moved to the National Cemetery near the Visitor's Center after the war. The Union troops did not take such good care of the Confederate dead. Union troops dug large trenches and stacked the Confederates allegedly sometimes up to seven deep. There are five known Confederate burial trenches, but there are probably many more that have never been found and are therefore lost to history.

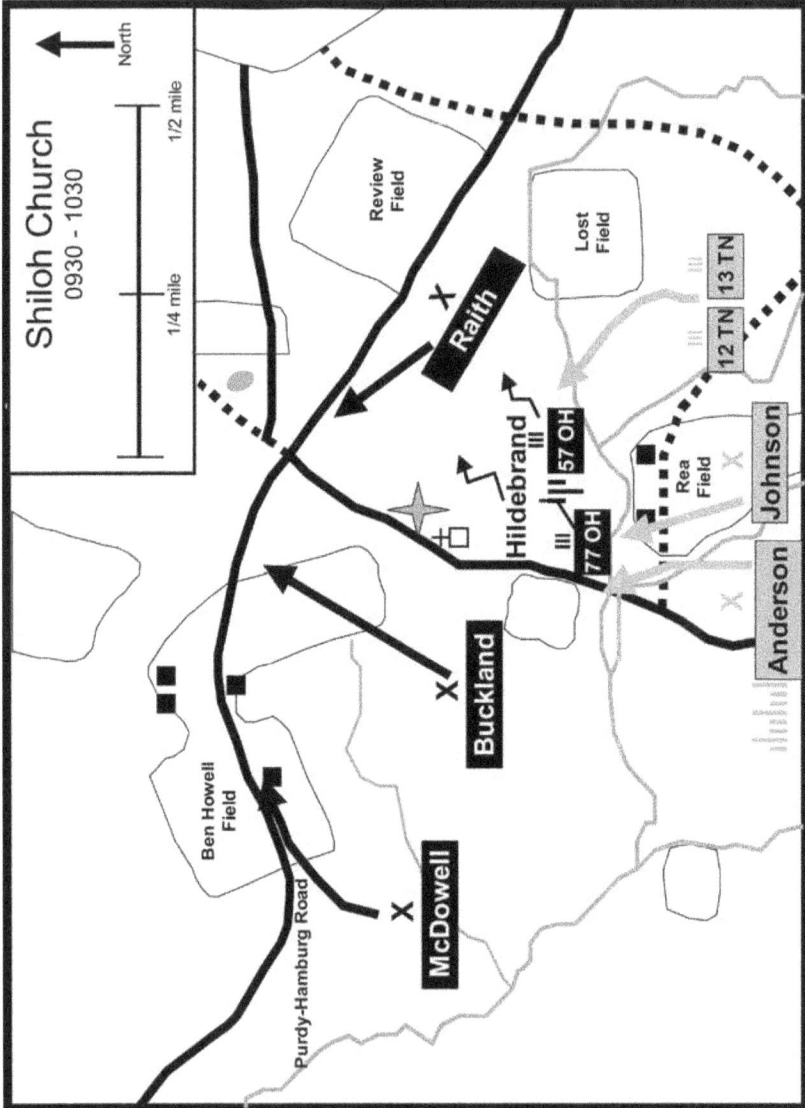

Shiloh Church
0930 - 1030

North

1/4 mile    1/2 mile

Review Field

Lost Field

Raith

Hildebrand

57 OH

77 OH

Rea Field

12 TN    13 TN

Johnson

Anderson

Buckland

McDowell

Ben Howell Field

Purdy-Hamburg Road

Map 9.

70

# Stand 4

## Shiloh Church

*Directions:* Continue northwest on Peabody Road for .1 mile. Turn right (north) at the triangle intersection. Travel .3 mile on Corinth Road and turn into the Shiloh Church parking lot. This is private property, but visitors are allowed without coordination. Move to the middle of the field to the east.

*Description:* During the fight on Rea Field, COL Ralph Buckland's 4th Brigade of Sherman's division held a line by its camps. By 0800 Buckland knew of the Confederate attacks and formed his brigade to the north of the flooded Shiloh Branch. The first Confederates to attack Buckland were the regiments of Cleburne's brigade that stayed west of Rea Field. Buckland easily drove them back. The Confederates had positioned 16 cannon to support the attack into Rea Field and west of Corinth Road. At 1000, after the Confederates had seized Rea Field, they continued their attack. Two regiments from Russell's brigade—the 12th and 13th Tennessee—swung in a wide arc to the east of Hildebrand's brigade. Additionally, men from Johnson's and Anderson's brigades pressed the attack frontally. As Russell's troops struck Hildebrand's flank, the Union troops started to break. First the 57th Ohio broke and headed for the landing. Waterhouse attempted to move his battery but lost four cannon to the charging Tennesseans. Soon the combined weight of the Confederate attack fell on the 77th Ohio, and it, too, broke for the rear. Sherman's left had now completely collapsed.

The Confederates now focused on Buckland's brigade west of Shiloh Church. Sherman had been all over the field that morning, rallying the men and coordinating the defense. As he saw Hildebrand's troops retreating, he determined his line was no longer tenable. He knew Buckland's flank was "in the air," so he ordered his division to fall back and establish a new line along the Purdy-Hamburg Road. Sherman dispatched staff officers and orderlies to deliver the message. Sherman's last brigade, the 1st, under COL John McDowell's command, had spent a relatively quiet morning. It had received sporadic artillery and sniper fire but no major Confederate attacks. McDowell received the order from one of Sherman's staff officers and easily withdrew to the north.

MG John McClernand, commander, 1st Division, also heard the firing south of his camps early in the morning. Sherman soon sent McClernand a request for aid, and McClernand formed his men. McClernand's camps were not tactically arranged either, so his three brigades were spread out. The 3d Brigade was the closest to Sherman's line. COL Leonard Ross commanded this brigade, but he was on leave for his wife's funeral. Acting Commander COL J. Reardon was sick and absent from the command that day, leaving COL Julius Raith in command. Upon receiving McClernand's orders, Raith posted his men behind Hildebrand's brigade. When Hildebrand broke, Raith was in position to stem the advancing Confederates, which his brigade did, at least for a while.

All along the line now, the Confederate attack stalled for about 30 minutes. Some of the units were exhausted; others were out of ammunition. Some units stopped to plunder Union camps. This Confederate pause was time for Sherman to reorganize his men in a new defensive position.

*Vignette:* A lieutenant in the 53d Ohio of Hildebrand's brigade describes his unit's leadership: "As I turned to go back from the left to the right, I saw the Fifty-seventh Ohio, which had been fighting on its color line, falling back through its camp, its ranks broken by the standing tents, despite the gallant efforts of its gallant lieutenant-colonel, A.V. Rice, the only field officer with it. I ran to where the colonel was lying on the ground behind a tree and stooping over said, 'Colonel, let us go and help the Fifty-seventh; they are falling back.' He looked up; his face was like ashes; the awful fear of death was on it; he pointed over his shoulder in an indefinite direction and squeaked out in a trembling voice: 'No, form the men back here.' Our miserable position flashed upon me. We were in the front of a great battle. Our regiment had never had a battalion drill. *Some men in it had never fired a gun.* Our lieutenant colonel had become lost in the confusion of the first retreat, the major was in the hospital, and our colonel was a coward! I said to him, with an adjective not necessary to repeat, 'Colonel, I will not do it!' He jumped to his feet and literally ran away." (Lieutenant Ephraim Dawes, 53d Ohio, in Ephraim C. Dawes, "My First Day Under Fire at Shiloh", *Sketches of War History*, vol. IV, Ohio Military Order of the Loyal Legion of the United States, 1903, 10-11.)

*Teaching point 1:* Leadership. For most of the unit leaders, this is their first action. Why do some leaders perform well and others cower? How do you prepare junior leaders for the reality of combat?

*Teaching point 2:* Battle command. Sherman's division is breaking. Sherman is all over the field encouraging the men and trying to maintain his unit's cohesiveness. How can Sherman best "fight" his division at this point in the battle?

*Teaching point 3:* Face of battle. For most of the soldiers, this is their first combat experience. How do you prepare soldiers for what they will see in combat? Why did the Confederate soldiers stop their attack when they were pushing the Union soldiers all along this line?

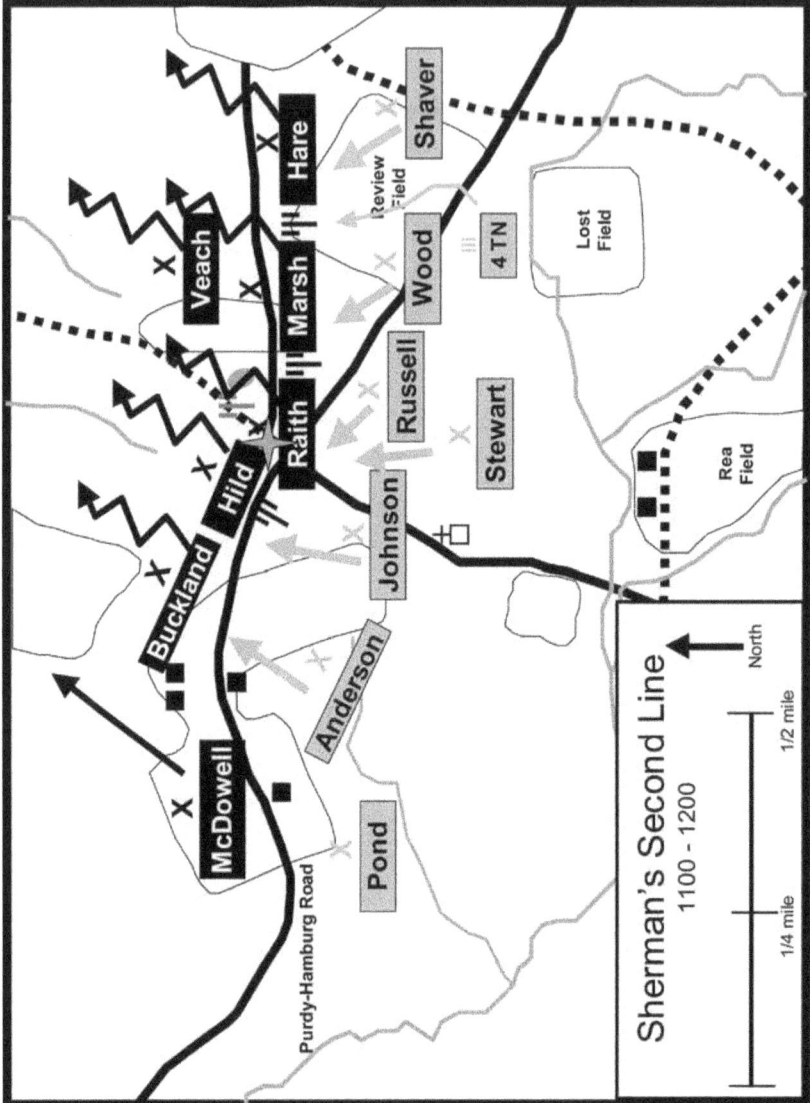

Map 10.

Sherman's Second Line
1100 - 1200

North

1/4 mile    1/2 mile

McDowell

Pond

Buckland

Anderson

Hild

Johnson

Raith

Russell

Stewart

Veach

Marsh

Hare

Wood

4 TN

Lost Field

Rea Field

Review Field

Shaver

Purdy-Hamburg Road

# Stand 5

## Sherman's Second Line

*Directions:* Travel north on Corinth Road for .2 mile. At the intersection, park and dismount. Move to the Raith death marker. You are at the intersection of Corinth Road and Hamburg-Purdy Road, also known as "the Crossroads."

*Description:* As Sherman's troops fell back, MG John McClernand was reacting. At Sherman's request he had organized his troops and moved forward. As COL A.M. Hare's and COL C.C. Marsh's brigades arrived north of the Purdy-Hamburg Road, McClernand halted them and formed a line of battle. He had Hare's brigade north of Review Field with Marsh's brigade west of Hare. McClernand sent a message to Raith and told him to fall back and form to the west of Marsh. Dispersed among McClernand's brigades were four artillery batteries. Once McClernand was set, COL James Veatch brought his brigade of Hurlbut's division forward in response to a request from Sherman. Veatch went into position behind Marsh.

As Sherman fell back, he tried to reform his lines. The disorganized survivors of Hildebrand's brigade were to the west of McClernand with Buckland to the west of Hildebrand. McDowell's brigade was still moving. As Buckland formed his troops in the road, the 6th Indiana Light Artillery Battery came flying past, scattering Buckland's troops. As Captain Frederick Behr brought the battery into position, the Confederates attacked. Behr was wounded, and his men broke for the rear without firing a shot.

By 1100 the Confederates were back in ranks and regained the initiative by resuming the attack. Fresh from the fight around Shiloh Church, the brigades of Anderson, Cleburne, Russell, and Johnson attacked Sherman and McClernand's right. Shaver and Wood, fresh from their fight against Prentiss, attacked McClernand's left. BG A.P. Stewart came up to join the attack. As he was trying to get in line, his 4th Tennessee Regiment became separated from the brigade. When Stewart found them, he received orders to seize Battery D, 1st Illinois Light Artillery in Review Field. Stewart moved out with the 4th Tennessee. The battery opened fire on Stewart's men, but the infantry support did not, thinking Stewart's men were friendly. When Stewart was 30 yards from the battery, he fired one volley and charged, capturing one piece as the battery withdrew. Stewart's other regiments attacked east of Russell.

As Stewart attacked, Wood's brigade came into the field and attacked

Marsh. Marsh held for a time, but one by one, the Federal regiments broke and retreated. The 14th Ohio Light Artillery Battery was in Marsh's line and was captured when Marsh retreated. Veatch's brigade, in line behind Marsh, could not open fire because Marsh's men were retreating through its ranks. The combination of Marsh's men and the Confederates soon had Veatch falling back as well. The center of McClernand's line was pierced. Soon after Wood defeated Marsh, Shaver's brigade attacked Hare. Hare's men did not stand long; they fired one volley and fled.

On the Confederate left, the brigades of Johnson, Russell, and Anderson attacked. Russell and Johnson attacked Raith as he was organizing, and Raith was shot in the leg as his line crumbled. Raith was left behind and died on 11 April. Anderson's brigade and part of Russell's fell on Sherman's confused line that was soon again retreating.

McDowell's brigade had not yet reached Sherman's new line when COL Preston Pond's brigade from Ruggles' division of Bragg's corps attacked him at Ben Howell Field. McDowell was holding Pond when he received a message from Sherman to retreat to the north. He was able to break contact and was soon heading north again.

The Confederates had now defeated Prentiss', Sherman's, and McClernand's divisions, but the pace of the battle was great and the Confederates again paused. Units from different corps were intermingled, men were exhausted and out of ammunition, and McClernand's camps were fresh for the taking. As Sherman and McClernand withdrew, they were not pursued.

***Vignette:*** Henry Stanley continued the attack with Shaver's brigade. He fell behind his unit, and as he tried to catch up, he found the debris of battle: "My company was not in sight. I was grateful for the rest, and crawled feebly to a tree, and plunging my hand into my haversack, ate ravenously. Within half an hour, feeling renovated, I struck north in the direction which my regiment had taken, over a ground strewn with bodies and the debris of war. . . . Close by . . . a young lieutenant, who, judging by the new gloss on his uniform, must have been some father's darling. A clean bullet hole through the center of his forehead had instantly ended his career. A little further were some twenty bodies, lying in various postures, each by its own pool of viscous blood, which emitted a peculiar scent, which was new to me, but which I have since learned is inseparable from a battlefield. Beyond these, a still larger group lay, body overlying body, knees crooked, arms erect, or wide-stretched and rigid, according as the last spasm overtook them. . . . For it was the first Field of Glory I had seen in my May of life, and the first time that Glory sickened me with its repulsive aspect, and made me suspect it was all a glittering lie." (Private Henry Stanley, 6th Arkansas, in Henry M. Stanley, *The Autobiography of Sir Henry Morton Stanley*, Cambridge, MA: Riverside Press, 1909, 194-95.)

*Teaching point 1:* Coordination. How are Sherman and McClernand coordinating their actions? Who should be coordinating these? How are the Confederate units coordinating? Who should be coordinating their attack?

*Teaching point 2:* Momentum. How could the Confederates have maintained their momentum? Was the loss of momentum critical at this point?

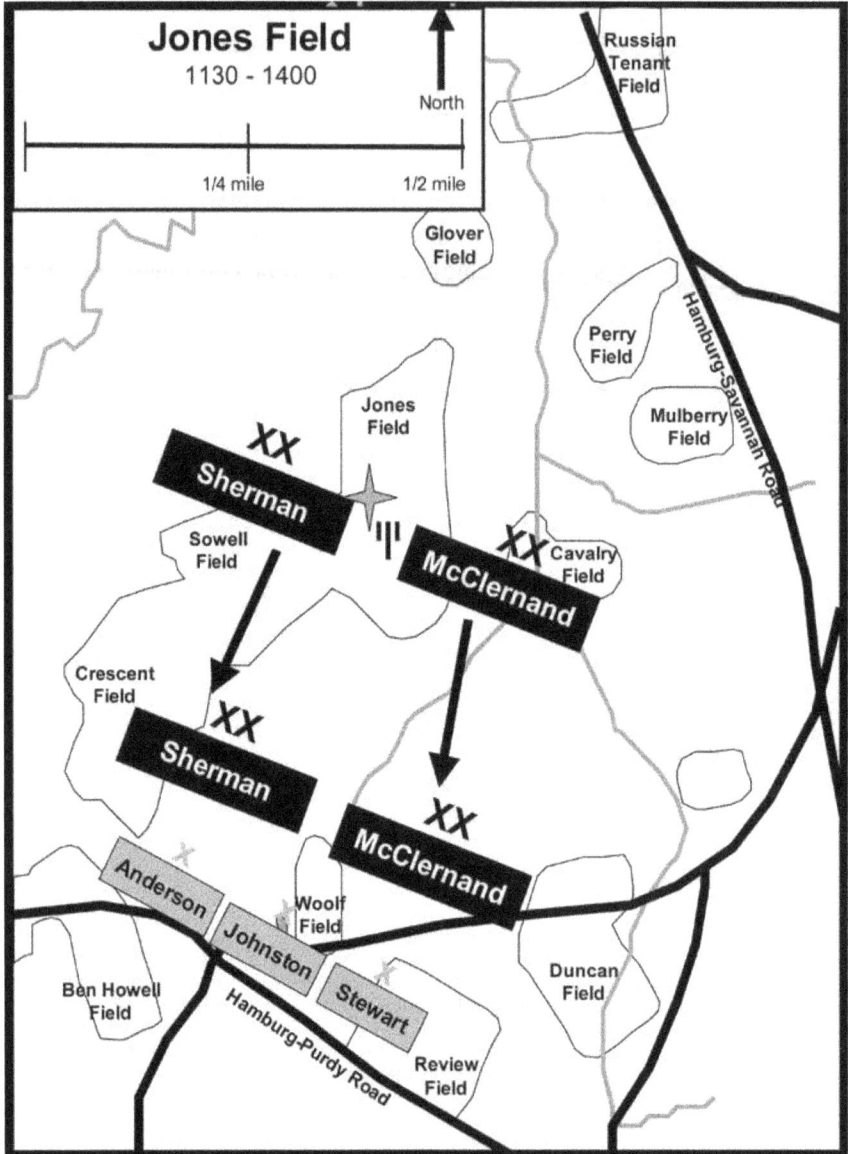

Map 11.

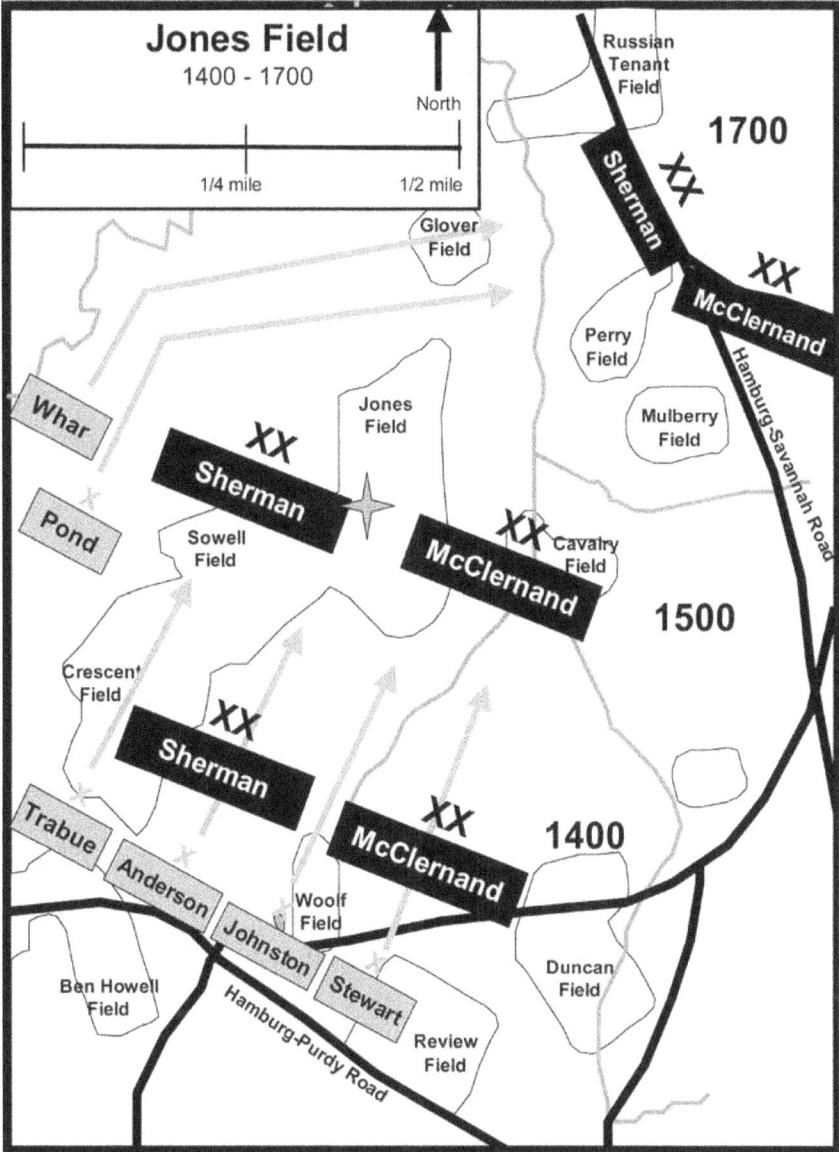

## Jones Field
### 1400 - 1700

North

1/4 mile     1/2 mile

Russian Tenant Field

1700

Sherman XX

McClernand XX

Glover Field

Perry Field

Mulberry Field

Hamburg-Savannah Road

Whar

Jones Field

Sherman XX

Pond

Sowell Field

McClernand XX

Cavalry Field

1500

Crescent Field

Sherman XX

McClernand XX

1400

Trabue

Anderson

Johnston

Woolf Field

Stewart

Ben Howell Field

Hamburg-Purdy Road

Review Field

Duncan Field

Map 12.

# Stand 6

## Jones Field

*Directions:* Go west on Hamburg-Purdy Road for .4 mile. Turn right (north) on TN 22 and go 1.1 miles. Pull off in the turnout by the Hare Headquarters Monument. Dismount and move to the cannon in the center of the field. You are now in Jones Field.

*Description:* Sherman's and McClernand's troops had fallen back in disarray in the vicinity of Jones Field. One of Sherman's brigades (Hildebrand) had been routed and left the field, another (Marsh) was greatly disorganized and trying to regroup, but McDowell's brigade was relatively fresh. McClernand's troops were also disorganized but regrouping, wisely using the time the Confederates had given them. The Confederates were still busy plundering captured camps and reorganizing after seizing Sherman's and McClernand's camps.

Sherman first placed a collection of nine cannons from three batteries in Jones Field to shell the Confederates. Sherman and McClernand met and decided that since their troops were intermingled and disorganized, they would divide the battlefield into sectors. Sherman would command on the right and McClernand on the left. Additionally, the two decided the time was right to counterattack the Confederates. At 1230 they attacked.

Sherman and McClernand's counterattack slammed into the unprepared Confederates. The Union troops drove the Confederates out of Marsh's captured camps and continued south until they reached Woolf Field where they halted and dressed the lines. Beauregard, Hardee, and Polk were surprised by this attack and moved to organize a defense. As Hardee and Polk formed their lines, Beauregard ordered his last Reserve brigade forward. COL Robert Trabue's brigade from the Reserve corps had been following the attack all morning and was fresh. Trabue's fresh regiments and other recently reorganized units fought the stubborn Union troops. At 1400, after almost 1 hour of close fighting, Sherman and McClernand's troops were near breaking and ordered to fall back to Jones Field again. The Confederates cautiously pursued.

The Union troops made a short stand in Jones Field but again decided to fall back. Earlier Sherman and McClernand had selected positions along the Hamburg-Savannah Road as a strong contingency position. The ground there was defensible, and Sherman wanted to secure the bridge over Snake Creek for Lew Wallace's division, which he expected to arrive soon.

As Sherman and McClernand formed their new line the Confederates launched an attack on the Union flank with Pond's brigade and a small cavalry battalion, COL John A. Wharton's Texas Rangers. Pond's men wore uniforms that the State of Louisiana issued, which were blue. As Pond formed, other Confederates mistakenly fired into his blue-clad men, causing casualties and disorganizing the unit. Once the unit recovered, Pond attacked but was repulsed. Wharton's Texas Rangers also attacked but were driven off.

Sherman and McClernand now were in a position with the Tennessee River at their backs. They could not withdraw much farther. Their counter-attack at 1200 had bought time for Grant and some of the other command-ers on the field. As the Union troops reorganized, many of the Confederate units they had been fighting moved to a new focal point—Union troops in the Hornet's Nest.

*Vignette:* The soldiers in Pond's brigade wore blue jackets that the State of Louisiana issued to them. On two occasions they were fired on by their own troops. COL Pond reported on the effects of this "friendly fire": "The left of the brigade was immediately thrown forward and the whole put in motion at double-quick to cut him off, and the movement would, without doubt, have been successful, but when nearly across the field a deadly fire was received from our own forces on the right, killing and wounding several of the Eighteenth Regiment Louisiana Volunteers, under the command of Colonel Mouton. Not knowing at first from whence the fire was directed, and feeling that I might have passed some of the enemy's forces, the brigade was halted and thrown back 100 yards, to the edge of the woods." COL Preston Pond, Brigade Commander, Ruggles' division, Bragg's corps, *The War of the Rebellion: A Compilation of the Official Records of the Union and Confederate Armies*, hereafter cited as *OR*, vol. 10, part 1, 517.)

*Teaching point 1*: Seizing the initiative. Were Sherman and McCler-nand correct in attacking, or should they have spent the time preparing a strong defensive position?

*Teaching point 2:* Reorganization. What was the effect of reorganiza-tion or a lack of it to the battle at this point?

*Teaching point 3:* Fratricide. What was the effect of fratricide on Pond's brigade? Could it have been prevented? How do we prevent it today?

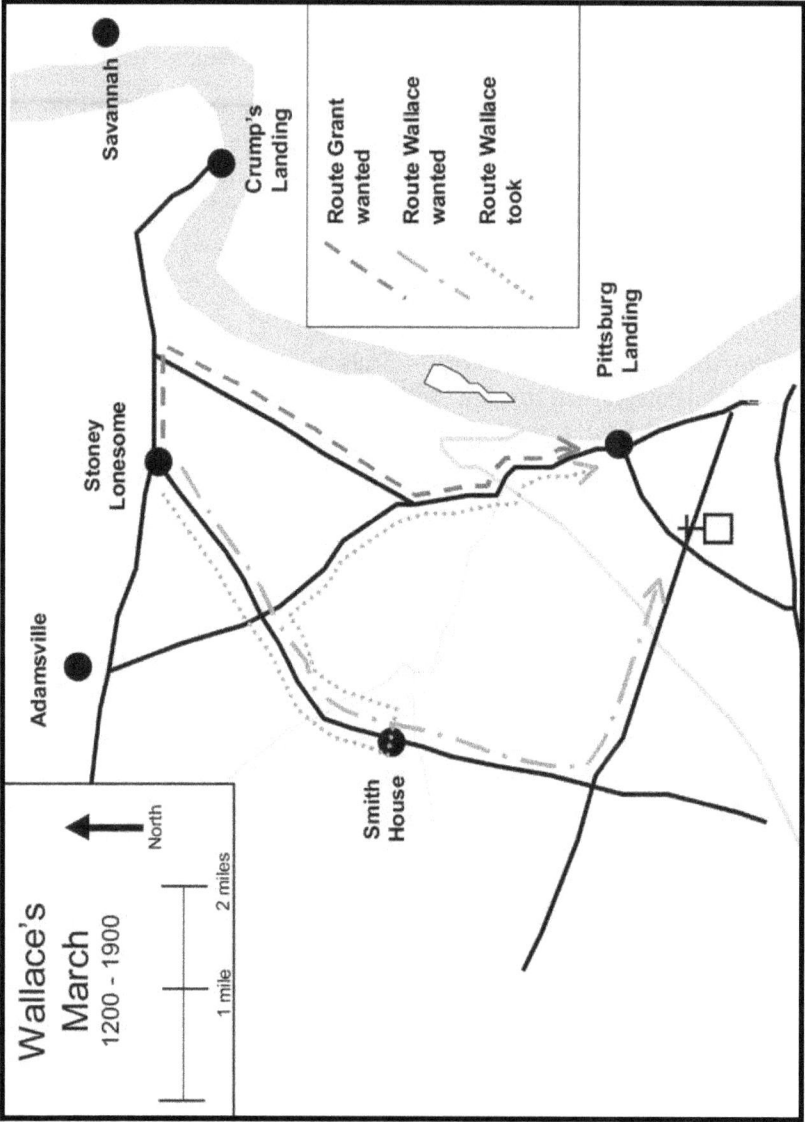

Wallace's March
1200 - 1900

North

1 mile    2 miles

Savannah

Crump's Landing

Route Grant wanted

Route Wallace wanted

Route Wallace took

Pittsburg Landing

Stoney Lonesome

Adamsville

Smith House

Map 13.

# Stand 7

## Lew Wallace's Division

*Directions:* Continue north on TN 22 for .5 mile. Turn right (east) toward the Visitor Center. Drive to the pullout 100 meters ahead, park, and dismount. Walk back toward the intersection and stop just short of it. The road across TN 22 is the road where Lew Wallace's division arrived.

*Description:* On 13 March 1862 Lew Wallace and his division dispatched from transports at Crump's Landing. His original mission was to damage the Mobile and Ohio Railroad at Bethel Station. Wallace had two battalions of cavalry assigned to his division. He sent the battalion from the 5th Ohio Cavalry to damage the railroad, and it eventually tore up 150 feet of trestle before returning to its camps (the Confederates repaired the damage the next day). While on the raid, the cavalry learned that there was a large Confederate force nearby, so Wallace was ordered to remain while the rest of the Army went into camp around Pittsburg Landing. Wallace disposed his troops with COL Charles Whittlesey's 3d Brigade at Adamsville, COL John Thayer's 2d Brigade at Stoney Lonesome, and COL Morgan Smith's 1st Brigade and division headquarters at Crump's Landing. Wallace was concerned because his division was isolated from the rest of the Army. Believing that any reinforcements coming to his aid would come from the end of the line (Sherman), Wallace decided to prepare the Shunpike, a small, dirt road, that ran from Sherman's camp to Stoney Lonesome. In late March Wallace had his cavalry recon and repair the Shunpike toward Sherman's camps.

At 0600, 6 April a sentinel woke Wallace and told him he heard firing to the south. Believing an attack to the south could mean a Confederate offensive, Wallace decided to concentrate his division at Stoney Lonesome in case the Confederates attacked from Purdy. He maintained a headquarters boat at Crump's Landing and moved there anticipating that orders would soon come. At 0830 Grant arrived at Crump's Landing aboard his headquarters boat, the *Tigress*. Grant did not disembark, but he moored to Wallace's boat and the two conferred across the rails of their respective boats. Grant told Wallace to be prepared to move to the south on a moment's notice. Wallace told Grant that he had already ordered his division concentrated and would wait for orders. When Grant left Wallace moved his headquarters to Stoney Lonesome. Before he departed he left a horse at Crump's Landing for any of Grant's staff officers who might arrive by boat with orders.

When Grant arrived at Pittsburg Landing and determined the seriousness of the situation, he ordered his Assistant Adjutant General Captain John Rawlins to send Chief Quartermaster Captain A.S. Baxter to Crump's Landing to order Wallace's division forward. When Rawlins gave Baxter the instructions, Baxter thought it best that orders be written, so Rawlins went on the *Tigress*, found a scrap of paper and a pencil, and drafted the orders. Baxter immediately departed on the *Tigress*, arriving at Crump's Landing at 1100. There he found the horse Wallace left and rode to Stoney Lonesome, arriving at 1130. Baxter handed the order to Wallace, who read it and said he was prepared to move. Baxter returned to the *Tigress*, and Wallace handed the order to one of his staff officers, Captain Frederick Knefler, who put it under his sword belt. Sometime during the day the orders fell out of the belt, an event that would haunt Wallace for the rest of his life.

After the battle there was a controversy about Wallace's movements to the battle. Grant and his staff officers said the order told Wallace to take "the road nearest to and parallel with the river." Wallace and his staff officers, however, said the order told them to "come up and take position on the right of the Army." Regardless, Wallace decided to move his division down the Shunpike as he had planned.

Baxter had given the order to Wallace at 1130, and after allowing his troops a quick meal (another decision drawing criticism later), Wallace was marching by 1200. Grant had expected Wallace to arrive quickly since he was only 5 miles away and throughout the day sent orderlies to hurry Wallace. One cavalry lieutenant reported that Wallace would not move unless he had written orders. Grant sent Captain W.R. Rowley of his staff to determine the situation with Wallace and to hurry him up.

Rowley found Wallace on the Shunpike at 1400. Rowley told Wallace that the cavalry lieutenant reported that Wallace would not move without written orders. "That's a damn lie!" was Wallace's response. Rowley then asked Wallace why he was using the Shunpike. Wallace responded that this was the route to Sherman and McClernand's camps. Rowley pulled Wallace aside and informed him that Sherman and McClernand had been pushed back almost to the river. Wallace was troubled by this news. Rowley then told Wallace that he was needed at Pittsburg Landing. Wallace countermarched his troops (instead of turning around he had the lead troops march back through the next in line). Wallace said he did this because he wanted his best troops in the front; but valuable time was lost.

Back at Pittsburg Landing Grant could not imagine what was keeping Wallace. At 1430 he sent Lieutenant Colonel James McPherson from his staff to hurry Wallace. Between 1530 and 1600 McPherson found Wallace. McPherson told Wallace that he was needed quickly and wondered why the lead elements were now halted. Wallace said he was allowing the trail elements time to close up because Grant "wanted the division, not part of it."

Lew Wallace did not arrive at the battlefield until after dark on 6 April. Due to the vague orders and Wallace's marching decisions, the 3d Division's 5,800 men did not fight that day. For the rest of his life Wallace would have to defend his actions on 6 April. Why did he take the Shunpike? Why did he let his soldiers eat before they marched? Why did he countermarch? Why was he so slow?

*Vignette:* Grant vented his feelings about Wallace in a letter written soon after the battle: "Had General Wallace been relieved from duty in the morning, and the same orders communicated to Brigadier General Morgan L. Smith (who would have been his successor), I do not doubt but the division would have been on the field of battle in the engagement before 10 o'clock of that eventful 6$^{th}$ of April. There is no estimating the difference this might have made in our casualties." (MG U.S. Grant to COL J.C. Kelton, 13 April 1863, in *O.R.*, vol. 10, part 1, 178.)

For the rest of his life Wallace had to defend his actions: "Apropos of my failure to get to the field Sunday, the first day of the battle, various statements have appeared in the earlier histories of the war. Some say I lost my way; others that I took the wrong road; others that the march was circuitous owing to a guide. Some deal with me in a friendly spirit; others maliciously. I give the facts, and beg to be judged by them." (Lew Wallace, *Lew Wallace: An Autobiography*, New York, 1906, 469.)

*Teaching point 1:* Clarity of orders. Could Wallace's confusion have been prevented? How do you ensure verbal orders are clear and concise?

*Teaching point 2:* Unit selection. Wallace could have just turned his men around when he changed routes. Instead, he had the lead brigade pass through the trailing units so he had the best brigade leading. Is it acceptable for commanders to select certain units for the "hard" missions?

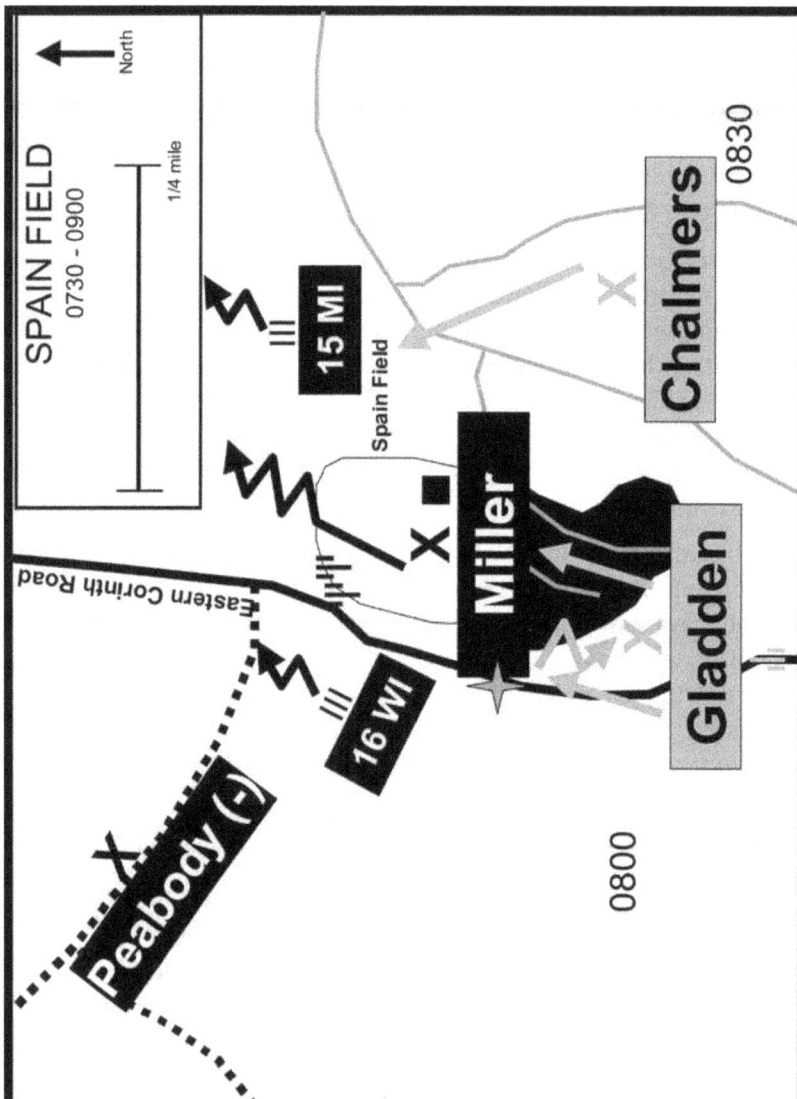

SPAIN FIELD
0730 - 0900

North

1/4 mile

15 MI

Spain Field

Miller

Chalmers
0830

Gladden

Eastern Corinth Road

16 WI

Peabody (-)

0800

Map 14.

# Stand 8

## Spain Field

We now shift to the actions on the Confederate right/Union left and go back to the early morning. This "jump in time" is required because of the road conditions in the park today.

*Directions:* Make a U-turn and head south on TN 22 for 3.3 miles. In the town of Shiloh, TN, 22 turns to the right, but you continue straight on TN 142 East for .3 mile past the intersection. Turn left (east) on Bark Road. After 1 mile, bear to the left (north) at the Y intersection (Bark Road becomes Gladden Road). Go .7 mile and park by the Gladden death marker. Spain Field is to your east.

*Description:* COL Madison Miller commanded the 2d Brigade of Prentiss' 6th Division. His brigade was composed of regiments that were newly arrived to the Army of the Tennessee. One had only joined the Army the previous day. Miller was having breakfast as his troops prepared for an inspection at 0900 when Prentiss rode rapidly into the camp shouting, "Colonel Miller, get out your brigade!" By 0730 Miller had formed his three regiments along the northern edge of Spain Field. Prentiss did not approve of the position and ordered Miller to advance to the southern edge of the field, which he did reluctantly. The 5th Ohio Battery and 1st Minnesota Battery unlimbered in the northwest corner of the field.

BG Adley H. Gladden commanded a brigade in BG Jones Withers' division of Bragg's corps. When the Army of the Mississippi formed for its attack, Gladden had been moved to Hardee's front line to cover the Army's flank along Lick Creek. Gladden advanced with the rest of the Army, but the difficult terrain ruined his alignment. Withers soon realized Gladden's troops could not extend all the way to Lick Creek, so he ordered BG James Chalmers' brigade from the second line to the first to extend his line to Lick Creek. At 0800 Gladden's troops approached Spain Field. The brigade quickly fell into disarray because of the swampy condition of the ground. Immediately, Miller's troops opened fire on Gladden. Gladden's troops slowly fell back and engaged in long-range firing with the Union troops.

Surprisingly, Prentiss ordered Miller to withdraw to his original position along the northern edge of the field because of Peabody's difficulties on Miller's right flank. As Miller fell back, the 15th Michigan Infantry arrived. They had reached Pittsburg Landing the day before and had been assigned to Prentiss' division. They advanced and took position on the left of Miller's line. Unfortunately, the 15th Michigan had never been issued ammunition! They went into the line armed only with bayonets.

Seeing the Union troops falling back, Gladden ordered a charge. As Gladden was watching the attack from his horse, a shell exploded over him, nearly severing his left arm. Gladden would die in Corinth on 12 April. Command of the brigade passed to COL Daniel Adams. Adams continued across the field, but the artillery's canister and the infantry's small-arms fire forced the Confederates back to the southern edge of the field.

In response, the Confederates brought up an artillery battery to duel with the Federal artillery. As soon as their fire was effective, Adams ordered another charge. The Confederate attack forced Miller's troops to retreat, leaving his artillery unsupported. One of the batteries lost two cannons, and both batteries were able to escape only through Herculean efforts.

Miller attempted to reform his regiments in their camps, but at 0830 Chalmers, brigade joined the fight on Gladden's (now Adams') right. Chalmers had a difficult time getting into position because of the rough terrain. Nevertheless, the combined attack broke Miller's brigade, and by 0900 Prentiss' division was shattered and streaming north toward Pittsburg Landing.

*Vignette:* A soldier in Gladden's brigade described the action: "The 21st Ala. & the 1st La. suffered more than any other Reg't engaged. Gen. Gladden's left arm was taken off about the first fire & Col. Adams of the 1st La. took com'd. Soon afterwards Maj. Armstead fell by a grape shot thro' his bowell [sic]. In a few minutes more Col. Deas rec'd a slight wound in his left hand. Then Col. Adams had his horse shot from under him while leading a charge. He soon rec'd a severe wound in the head & Col. Deas took command of the brigade & not long afterwards had his horse killed & rec'd a wound in his—arm & one, I beleive [sic], in his hip, tho' neither of them at all serious. On both sides the slaughter was heavy until the Com'd to charge was given & as soon as our columns began to move the enemy fled & our forces took possession of their camp. Here was a perfect curiosity shop. Every thing in the eating & wearing line, in fact every tent told of high & extravagant living." (Sergeant Horatio Wiley, 22d Alabama Infantry in Horatio Wiley, letter to "My Dear Josie," 11 April 1862 in the collection of the Northeast Mississippi Museum Association, Corinth, Mississippi.)

*Teaching point 1:* Succession of command. What was the effect of

88

Gladden's death? How do you prepare for a change of commander during a fight?

*Teaching point 2:* Battle command. Was Prentiss a help or a hindrance? Should he have ordered Miller to change positions?

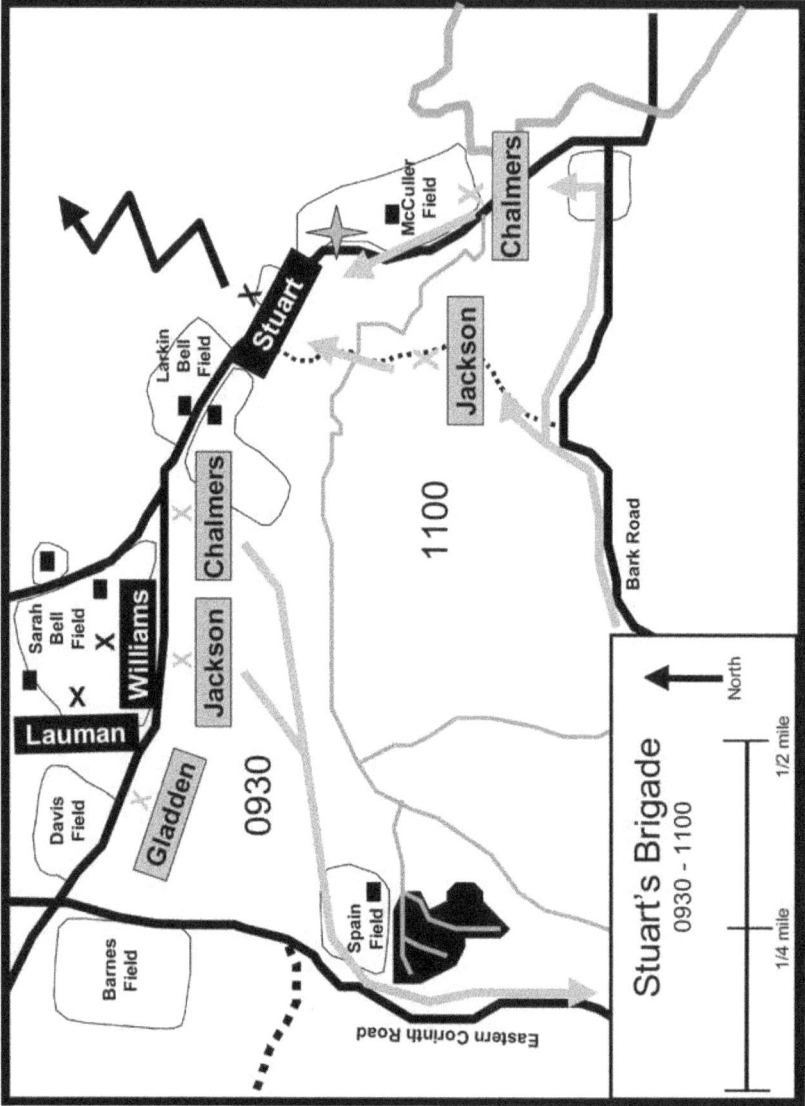

Map 15.

Stuart's Brigade
0930 - 1100

North

1/4 mile    1/2 mile

# Stand 9

## Stuart's Brigade

*Directions:* Continue north on Gladden Road for .1 mile. Bear right (north) on Eastern Corinth Road for .5 mile. Turn right (east) on Hamburg-Purdy Road for .7 mile. Turn into the service road on the left and stop by Stuart's Headquarters Monument. You are now in Larkin Bell Field.

*Description:* When Sherman disembarked his division at Pittsburg Landing on 17 March he took most of his troops to the vicinity of Shiloh Church. Sherman left COL David Stuart's 2d Brigade to guard the Lick Creek ford on the Hamburg-Savannah Road. Stuart placed his three regiments in camps around Larkin Bell Field.

After routing Miller's brigade at Spain Field, Chalmers continued his attack. BG John K. Jackson was ordered to bring his men up from the second line to fill a gap that had occurred between Gladden and Chalmers. These brigades now approached the Union troops around Sarah Bell's Cotton Field.

Early in the day Bragg had sent his engineer, Captain Samuel Lockett, to conduct a reconnaissance of the Union left. Lockett found Stuart's brigade around Larkin Bell Field and concluded that it was a Union division. Concerned for the safety of the Confederate right flank, Lockett sent messages to General Johnston informing him of this Union "division." Johnston immediately sent a message to Beauregard telling him to send Breckinridge's corps to the right. Johnston also sent an order to Chalmers and Jackson to disengage and move to the right. At 0930 Chalmers and Jackson easily broke contact and took the Bark Road to the right.

Stuart heard the firing to the west early in the morning, and when Prentiss sent him a message that he was under attack, Stuart put his men in the line of battle. He placed skirmishers at the ford and along Locust Grove Run. Stuart spread the rest of his brigade on the line from McCuller Field to Larkin Bell Field. Having sent his battery away as part of the artillery reorganization, he had no artillery.

At 1000 Jackson and Chalmers began forming their lines. Additionally, they placed an artillery battery to support their advance. At 1100 they attacked. Stuart's brigade performed poorly from the start. His right regiment broke quickly when faced with Jackson's advancing troops. On the left the units put up a little better fight, but they were soon routed and fled to the rear. Stuart was wounded while trying to rally his men.

The Confederates had mostly cleared the Union troops from the right (Union reinforcements were approaching), but a path to Pittsburg Landing was open. All the Confederates had to do was reinforce the attack and they would accomplish their plan of turning the Union Army away from Pittsburg Landing. With victory in their grasp, the Confederates faltered. Chalmers' men were out of ammunition, and there were no ordnance wagons nearby. Jackson's men plundered Stuart's camps and could not be reformed; Breckinridge's corps had not arrived at the right.

*Vignette:* On 7 April Dr. B.J.D. Irwin, 4th Division, Army of the Ohio, established one of the first ever tent field hospitals. He recounted: "During the military movements of troops during the battle of Shiloh, one of the operating hospitals was moved forward to a deserted farmhouse situated on an open piece of unbroken ground. The presence of a spring of cool potable water and the nearness of the building to a branch of the creek were advantages that were promptly recognized. . . . The proximity of this field hospital to the recaptured camp of a division of our troops defeated and made prisoner the preceding day, suggested the utilization of the abandoned tents for the benefit of the wounded; and as soon as the battle ceased the hospital tents, commissary tents, and wall tents pertaining thereto were accordingly taken possession of, and in short space of time were removed to and pitched in regular order on the level ground by which the house was surrounded. The building afforded an operating room, dispensary, office, kitchen, and dining room. Long into the night the ambulances continued to bring in the wounded, who, after receiving the necessary professional attendance, were made as comfortable as possible being supplied with an abundance of warm food, good bedding, and shelter from inclement weather. Next day the hospital camp was enlarged as to accommodate 300 patients, and the tents were systematically arranged; all bedsteads, cots, bedding, cooking and messing utensils, hay and straw found in the abandoned camp were taken possession of, and on the evening of the 8th the Division Medical Purveyor reached us with our medical supplies and hospital stores. . . . It soon became manifest that the wounded in this improvised field hospital were better provided for and more comfortable in every way than those who were moved aboard the hospital transports." (Report of Dr. B.J.D. Irwin in *Medical and Surgical History of the War of the Rebellion*, vol. II, part III, 1883, 921-22.)

*Teaching point 1:* Reconnaissance. Should the Confederates have known the disposition of the Union left before the battle? What was the effect of Lockett's report of a division?

*Teaching point 2:* Reserves. Was Breckinridge's corps in the correct position? Were the Confederate dispositions faulty if the plan was to turn the Union left?

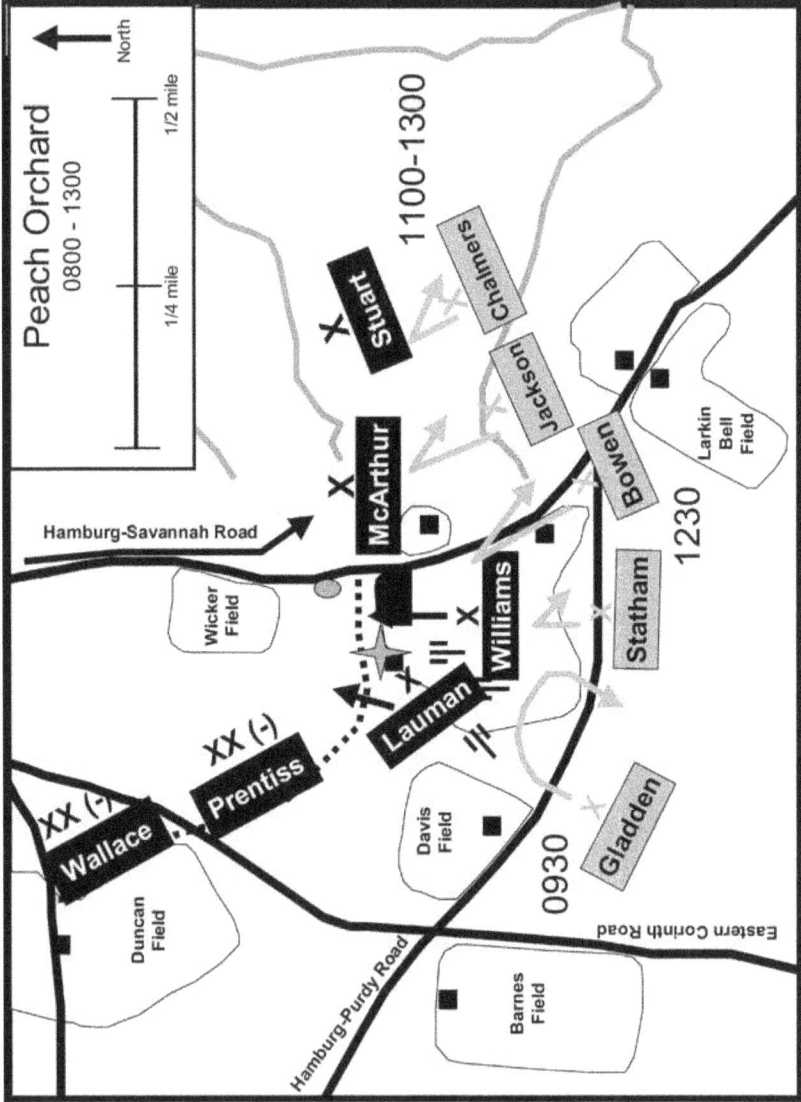

Peach Orchard
0800 - 1300

North

1/4 mile    1/2 mile

Hamburg-Savannah Road

Wicker Field

Duncan Field

Hamburg-Purdy Road

XX (-)
Wallace

XX (-)
Prentiss

Davis Field

Barnes Field

Eastern Corinth Road

0930

McArthur

Lauman

Williams

Gladden

Statham

1230

Bowen

Jackson

Chalmers

Stuart

1100-1300

Larkin Bell Field

Map 16.

94

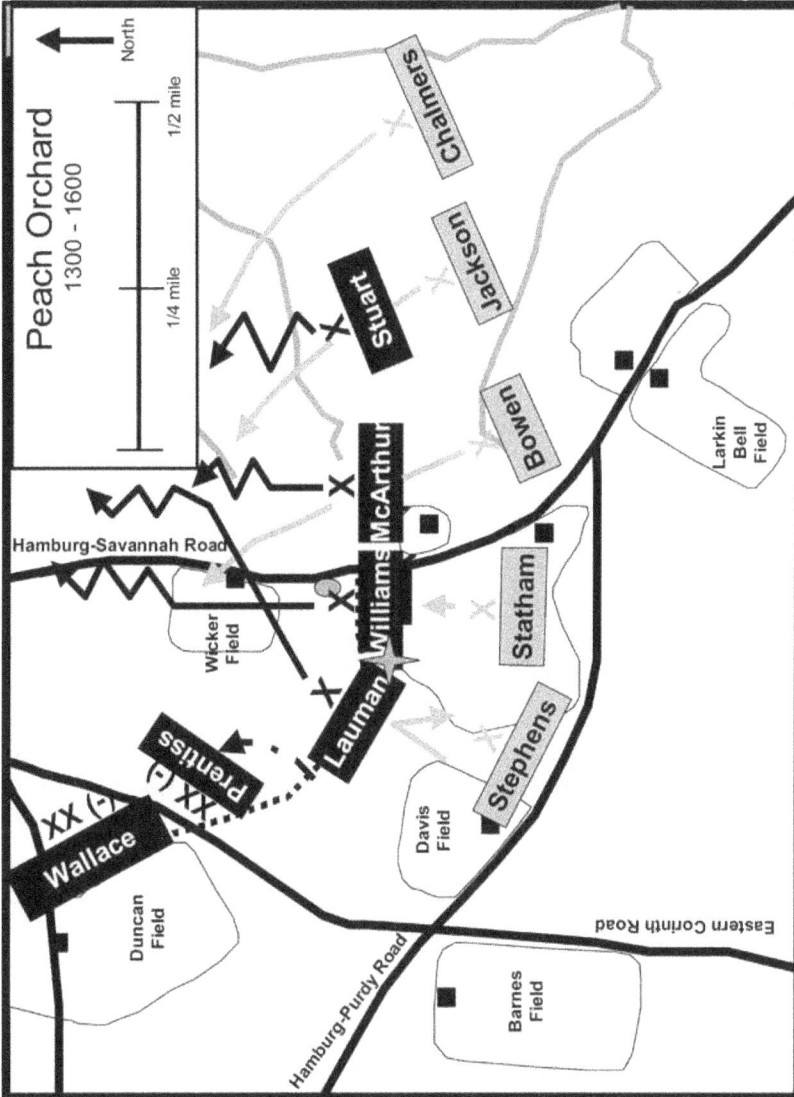

# Peach Orchard
## 1300 - 1600

North

1/4 mile   1/2 mile

Chalmers

Jackson

Stuart

Bowen

Williams McArthur

Larkin Bell Field

Hamburg-Savannah Road

Wicker Field

Statham

Lauman

Prentiss

Stephens

XX (-)
Wallace

Davis Field

Duncan Field

Eastern Corinth Road

Hamburg-Purdy Road

Barnes Field

Map 17.

95

# Stand 10

## The Peach Orchard

*Directions:* Depart the service road and bear right (north) on Hamburg-Savannah Road for .2 mile. Turn right (east) toward Johnston's death marker. Dismount and walk west across the road into Sarah Bell Field.

Depart the service road and turn right (north) on Hamburg-Savannah Road for .2 mile. Turn left (west) into the parking lot. Dismount and walk to the W. Manse George cabin. Sarah Bell Field is to your south, and the Peach Orchard is to your east.

*Description:* At 0730 Sherman sent a request for assistance to BG Stephen A. Hurlbut, commander of the 4th Division. Hurlbut dispatched his 2d Brigade under COL James Veatch and formed his remaining two brigades in the vicinity of their camps. At 0800 Hurlbut received another request for aid, this time from Prentiss. Hurlbut immediately had his command on the Hamburg-Savannah Road. As Hurlbut's men advanced, they ran into survivors from Prentiss' division who were full of tales of despair and doom. Hurlbut immediately ordered his men into line where they were, in Sarah Bell Field. COL Nelson Williams formed his 1st Brigade facing south while BG Jacob G. Lauman formed on Williams' right and oriented west. Hurlbut assigned a battery to each infantry brigade and placed a third, his best, at the seam between the infantry units.

Three Confederate brigades—Gladden (now under Deas), Jackson, and Chalmers—formed to attack. The Confederates unlimbered a battery, and one of its first shots wounded Williams, who was replaced by COL Isaac Pugh. The Confederate battery also caused one of the Union batteries to break and run. At 0930 the three Confederate brigades began their attack. Before they could get far a staff officer from Johnston ordered Jackson and Chalmers to move to the right to attack the Union "division" there. Gladden's brigade, however, continued the attack. It ran into Lauman's troops and soon drifted to the east, right in front of Williams' brigade. Soon, the Confederates were retreating, but Pugh, fearing an attack on his left flank, ordered his men to the north side of the field. Hurlbut had no choice but to withdraw Lauman as well.

At the moment, Gladden's brigade was the only Confederate brigade fronting Sarah Bell Field, and there was a pause in the action. Prentiss used this time to rally some individual regiments and formed them on the right of Hurlbut. Again, the Federals gained valuable time during the Confederates' suspended action.

When Johnston had ordered Jackson and Chalmers to the right he also instructed Beauregard to send the Reserve corps to the right. Breckinridge brought up two of his three brigades (the third had been sent to the Confederate left). Additionally, COL William H. Stephens' brigade from Polk's corps, badly depleted after an assault on the Hornet's Nest (which we will discuss at the next stand), moved into position south of Sarah Bell Field.

About 1030 Union BG John McArthur brought part of his brigade (three of the five regiments were detached) from W.H.L. Wallace's division to the Union left and went into position on Hurlbut's left. The survivors of Stuart's brigade formed on McArthur's left. At 1100 Jackson and Chalmers, fresh from routing Stuart's brigade, attacked McArthur and Stuart. For the next 2 hours, they tried to defeat the Union troops but were unsuccessful in every attack. At 1230 BG John Bowen's brigade and COL Winfield Statham's brigade of Breckinridge's Reserve corps joined the attack. The attacks were all uncoordinated and piecemeal, and therefore were unsuccessful.

At 1330 Breckinridge told Johnston that his men would not attack anymore. Johnston rode around the lines encouraging the men and coordinating the attack. At 1400 everything was finally ready for a coordinated attack. Five Confederate brigades—Stephens, Statham, Bowen, Jackson, and Chalmers—attacked. Leading this attack were the highest-ranking field general in the Confederacy, Johnston; former Vice President of the United States Breckinridge; and the Governor of Tennessee, Isham G. Harris.

On the Confederate left, Stephens' brigade met a terrible fire from the Union troops. The troops pressed on, but the fire was too much and Stephens' men retreated. Statham's men entered the field and were able to push Hurlbut's men back but could not break them. On the Confederate right, the combined efforts of Bowen's and Jackson's men were too much for the battered men of Stuart's brigade who retreated. McArthur's flank was now exposed, and the Confederates exploited this. Soon McArthur was falling back, exposing Hurlbut's flank. McArthur and Stuart tried to rally their men, but both were wounded and their brigades fled. Hurlbut's troops fell back to Wicker Field, but with three Confederate brigades poised to attack their flank, the men did not hold and started to retreat.

Prentiss' survivors now had their left flank exposed. Prentiss refused his flank, and the men formed a new line facing east. The way to Pittsburg Landing was again open, but the Confederates slowly started to surround the Union troops to the west.

*Vignette:* Separated from his regiment and fighting with McArthur's brigade, 16-year-old musician John A. Cockerill stopped to help a comrade during the retreat: "Just by my side ran a youthful soldier, perhaps three years my senior, who might, for all I knew, have been recruited as I was. I heard him give a scream of agony, and, turning, saw him dragging one of his legs, which I saw in an instant had been shattered by a bullet. He had dropped his rifle, and as I ran to his support he fell upon my shoulder and begged me for God's sake to help him. I half carried him for some distance. . . . All this time, the bullets were whistling more fiercely than at any time during the engagement, and the woods were filled with flying men, who, to all appearances, had no intention of rallying on that side of the Tennessee River. My companion was growing weaker all the while, and finally I set him down beside a tree, with his back toward the enemy, and watched him for a few moments, until I saw that he was slowly bleeding to death. I knew nothing of surgery at that time and did not even know how to staunch the flow of blood. I called to a soldier who was passing, but he gave no heed. A second came, stood for a moment, simply remarked, 'He's a dead man' and passed on. I saw the poor fellow die without being able to render the slightest assistance." (John A. Cockerill, "A Boy at Shiloh," published in C.R. Graham, *Under Both Flags: A Panorama of the Great Civil War*, San Francisco: J. Dewing Co., 1896, 368.)

*Teaching point 1:* Synchronization. Did the Confederates have enough combat power to defeat the Union troops at this location? If so, why did it take them so long?

*Teaching point 2:* Battle command. Was Johnston commanding the Army well? Should he have coordinated the attacks sooner?

# Stand 11

## Johnston's Death

*Directions:* Recross the road (east) toward Johnston's death marker and walk toward the gully southeast of the marker.

*Description:* Johnston had been active the entire morning. He spent most of his time on the Confederate right, supervising activities there. At 0900 he rode into the recently captured camp of Miller's brigade. Seeing a Confederate officer carrying an armful of trophies, Johnston clamored, "None of that sir; we are not here for plunder!" Johnston regretted the strong rebuke and picking up a tin cup said, "Let this be my share of the spoils today."

After ordering Jackson and Chalmers to the far right, Johnston moved there. Early in the afternoon Breckinridge rode to Johnston and told him he had could not get his men to make a charge. Johnston rode in front of BG John Bowen's brigade, and with the tin cup he had "captured," Johnston tapped the soldiers' bayonets and told them, "I want you to show General Breckinridge and General Bragg what you can do with your bayonets and tooth picks."

At one point Johnston led an attack part of the way. During the charge, his uniform was shot through, and the sole of one of his boots was shot partially away. He was also nicked in the shoulder. After the attack, Johnston told Tennessee Governor Harris, a volunteer aide, "Governor, they came very near putting me hors de combat in that charge."

At 1415 Harris, recently returned from carrying on an order from Johnston, looked over at the army commander and noticed that he was pale and ready to fall from the saddle. Harris rode over, grabbed Johnston, and asked, "General, are you wounded?" Johnston replied, "Yes and I fear seriously." Harris, with the help of other staff officers, moved Johnston to the cover of the gully and took him from his horse. The staff officers ripped open Johnston's coat and shirt trying to find the wound. BG William Preston was a Johnston staff officer who was also his brother-in-law. Preston held Johnston's head and yelled, "Johnston, don't you know me?" At 1430 Johnston was dead.

Johnston had been shot in the back of the right knee. The bullet had severed an artery in his leg. Johnston had earlier dispatched his personal surgeon to help with the massive number of wounded. Ironically, the general had a life-saving tourniquet in his pocket, but no one knew about it. The exact time that Johnston was wounded is unknown. Johnston had very poor sensation in his right leg because of an old dueling wound. He may have been hit while leading the charge or by a stray shot later. Who fired the shot is also unknown. The fatal bullet came from an Enfield rifle, a weapon that both sides used on this part of the field.

Members of Johnston's staff wrapped his body, hiding his identity so his loss would not damage morale and started it back to Corinth. Staff officers quickly rode to Beauregard at the intersection of the Pittsburg-Corinth Road and Purdy-Hamburg Road and told him of Johnston's death. Beauregard was now commander of the Army of the Mississippi.

*Vignette:* Governor Harris recalled telling Beauregard of Johnston's death: "Immediately after the death of Albert Sydney Johnston I hurriedly sought out General Beauregard, whom I found sitting on his horse at Shiloh Church, and to whom I reported the death of General Johnston. General Beauregard said nothing in reply to my announcement for some moments but seemed to be in a deep study. He then said, 'Well Governor, everything is progressing well, is it not?' I answered that it was as far as my observation extended and then turned my horse and rode away." (W.B. Ellis, "Who Lost Shiloh to the Confederacy?" *Confederate Veteran*, vol. 22, 1914, 313.)

*Teaching point 1:* Commander's location. Should Johnston have been leading charges and placing himself in such a dangerous position? Should Johnston have been a commander or a leader (and what is the difference)?

*Teaching point 2:* First aid. Could Johnston's death have been prevented? How do you have enough medically trained personnel without reducing the number of fighters?

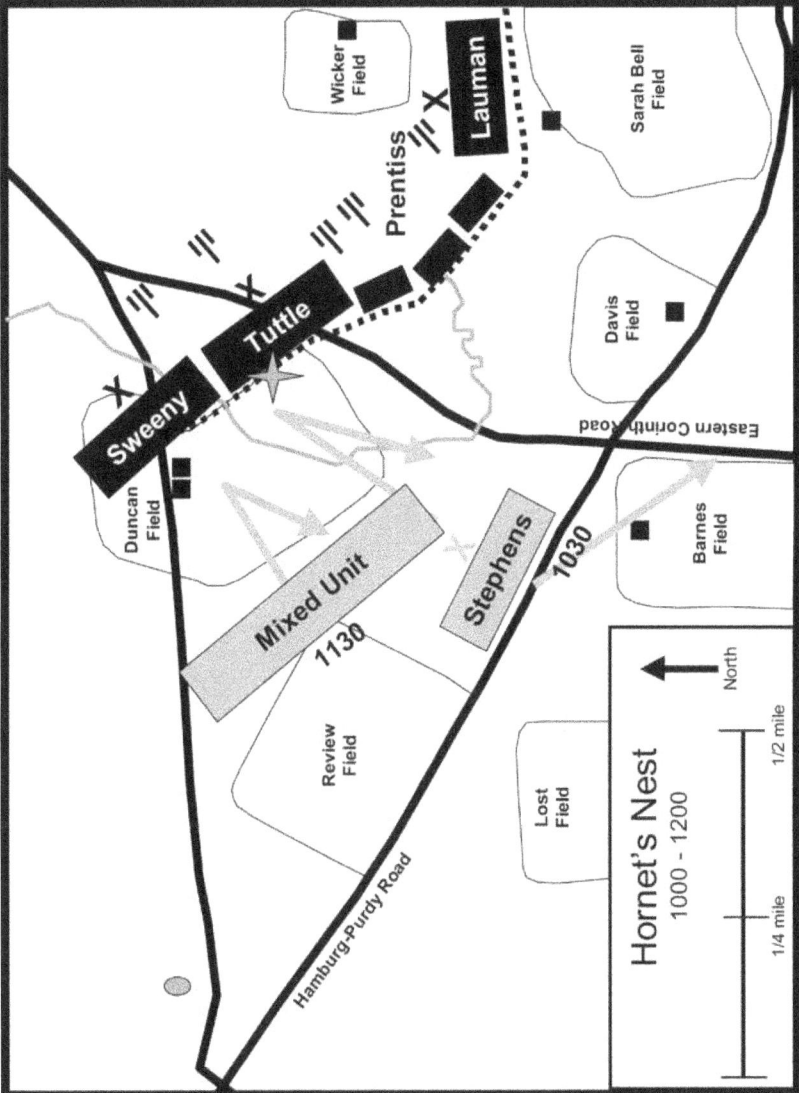

Wicker Field

Lauman

Prentiss

Sarah Bell Field

Tuttle

Davis Field

Sweeny

Duncan Field

Eastern Corinth Road

Mixed Unit

Stephens

1030

Barnes Field

1130

Review Field

Hamburg-Purdy Road

Lost Field

Hornet's Nest
1000 - 1200

North

1/4 mile        1/2 mile

Map 18.

101

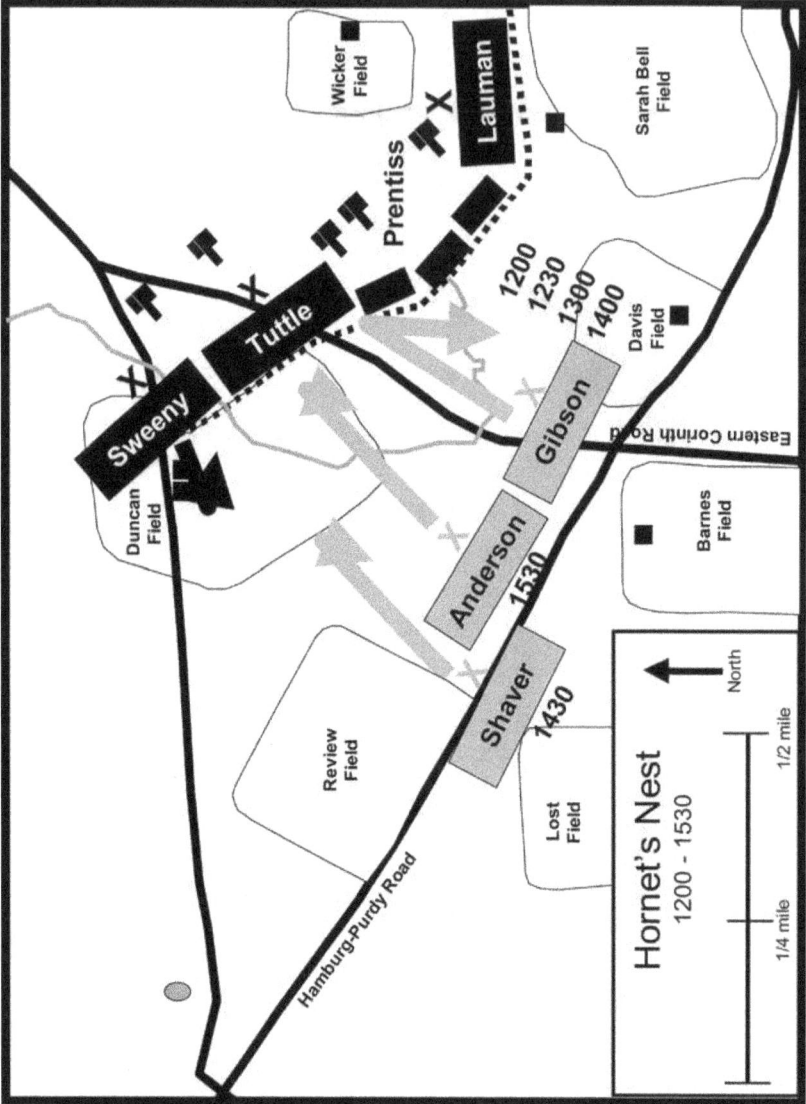

Map 19.

Hornet's Nest
1200 - 1530

North

1/2 mile    1/4 mile

Wicker Field

Lauman

Prentiss

Sarah Bell Field

Tuttle

Sweeny

Duncan Field

1200
1230
1300
1400

Davis Field

Gibson

Eastern Corinth Road

Anderson

1530

Barnes Field

Shaver

1430

Review Field

Lost Field

Hamburg-Purdy Road

102

# Stand 12

## The Hornet's Nest

*Directions:* Depart the parking lot and turn left (north) on Hamburg-Savannah Road. Bloody Pond is on your left. (During the battle, wounded soldiers of both sides, in an attempt to quench their thirst, made their way to this pond. Their blood turned the water red, and it has forever been known as "Bloody Pond.") Travel .7 mile on Hamburg-Savannah Road. Turn left (southwest) on Corinth-Pittsburg Landing Road for .5 mile. Park at the pullout on the right. Dismount and walk east on the Sunken Road, over the bridge to the 7th Iowa Monument. You are on the Sunken Road looking into Duncan Field. The Sunken Road was a farm road that had settled lower than the surrounding terrain because of the excessive weight of the farmer's wagons that traveled the road.

*Description:* After dispatching McArthur's brigade to the Union left, BG W.H.L. Wallace had the remaining two brigades of his division on the road by 0900. He moved his men forward and formed on Hurlbut's right along a slightly sunken road that bordered Duncan Field. Wallace placed COL Thomas G. Sweeny's understrength brigade (only two regiments; the rest were in reserve and were sent to the Union left) to the right and COL James Tuttle's brigade to the left. Wallace was in position behind a brush-covered fence at 1000. Soon survivors from Prentiss' division filled in a gap between Wallace and Hurlbut.

At 0920 Beauregard, while moving his headquarters, spotted COL William Stephens' brigade of Cheatham's division and Polk's corps. Beauregard ordered Cheatham to move the brigade toward the center of the line. At 1000 Cheatham had Stephens in position on the west end of Duncan Field. Observing Union troops across the field, Cheatham ordered a charge. Stephens' brigade was slaughtered as it crossed the field; Union artillery and infantry fire tore large gaps in the lines. Stephens' men made it halfway across the field before they had to retreat. Stephens withdrew and moved to the Confederate right.

By 1100 the Confederate corps commanders realized that corps integrity was lost. Bragg and Polk decided on their own to divide the battlefield into sectors: Bragg would command the right, Polk the center, and Hardee the left. Each corps commander would command the troops in his sector regardless of their original organization. At 1130 3,500 Confederate troops from four brigades—all of Shaver's and parts of Cleburne's, Wood's, and Stewart's) made a second attack. Their line stretched from Eastern Corinth Road to Corinth Road. This second attack faltered along the edge of the field.

After reorganizing the command structure, Bragg found COL Randal L. Gibson's brigade from BG Daniel Ruggles' division. Bragg immediately ordered Gibson to attack. At 1200 Gibson formed his four regiments and advanced. Unfamiliar with the terrain, Gibson advanced his men through a thicket by a streambed. The men stumbled forward through the rough terrain until they were right on top of the Union line. Suddenly the Union troops arose and blasted Gibson's men. Almost immediately the survivors of this "ambush" retreated in haste.

At 1215 Grant and his escort arrived at Prentiss' location. After receiving Prentiss' report, Grant told him to "maintain that position at all hazards." Grant additionally promised that Lew Wallace's division would soon arrive.

As soon as Gibson had fallen back, Bragg immediately ordered the brigade to try again. Many troops and leaders thought it was suicide, but they followed orders. At 1230 Gibson attacked again along the same line. Gibson's troops reached the Union lines and fighting was hand to hand. Local Union counterattacks and effective canister fire forced Gibson back again. A fire broke out in front of the Union positions, and many wounded men who could not escape burned to death in front of the Union troops who were powerless to rescue them.

As Gibson withdrew for a second time, some of the regimental commanders recommended to Bragg that they try to flank the position. Bragg would have none of that and ordered Gibson to make a third attack. Gibson and his regimental commanders led the men back across the field at 1300 and again were repulsed. Major James Powell, the leader of the patrol that started the battle that morning in Fraley Field, was mortally wounded during this attack.

For a fourth time Bragg ordered Gibson back across the field. Apparently enraged that the attacks had all failed, Bragg sent staff officers to the regiments to encourage them, aggravating their commanders. At 1400 Gibson's troops attacked Sunken Road for the fourth time. By this stage of the battle, Gibson's men had become demoralized, and the attack ended very soon after it started. During these attacks, Gibson lost more than 25 percent of his men, whose bodies now littered Duncan Field and adjoining woods.

At 1430 Bragg located COL R.G. Shaver who was in command of Hindman's brigade of Hardee's corps. Bragg ordered him to assault the Sunken Road. Shaver's troops slammed into Tuttle and Prentiss and soon retreated.

COL Sweeny, encouraged by the Confederate repulses, led his two regiments across Duncan Field and ran into the eighth Confederate assault in that spot for the day. This time BG Patton Anderson's brigade from Ruggles' division of Bragg's corps attacked. Like the seven previous attacks, this one also failed.

From 1030 to 1530 the Confederates had attacked the Union troops of W.H.L. Wallace and Prentiss along the Sunken Road eight times. All of the attacks were uncoordinated, had minimal artillery support, and were piecemeal. The fire was so severe that the Confederates said the fire reminded them of hornets flying by their heads. They would forever call this part of the field the Hornet's Nest. At 1530 the Union troops in the center were still holding on, but over the next few hours, the situation would change.

*Vignette:* Captain Andrew Hickenlooper, 5th Ohio Light Artillery described the action in the Hornet's Nest: "Quickly came the orders sharp and clear: 'Shrapnel,' 'Two seconds,' 'One second,' 'canister.' Then, as the enemy made preparations for their final dash, 'double canister' was delivered with such rapidity that the separate discharges blended into one continuous roar. Then the supporting infantry, rising from their recumbent position, sent forth a sheet of flame and leaden hail that elicited curses, shrieks, groans and shouts, all blended into an appalling cry. . . . Again and again, through long and trying hours, this dance of death went on, at frequent intervals, from 9 in the morning until 4 in the afternoon, thus gradually sapping the energies of these heroic men, who had borne the heat and burden of the fateful day with a courage unparalleled in the annals of the Civil War." (Andrew Hickenlooper, "The Battle of Shiloh," *Sketches of War History*, vol. V, Wilmington, NC: Broadfoot Publishing Co., 1903, 420).

*Teaching point 1:* Mass and synchronization. How did this small Union force defeat eight attacks by five Confederate brigades? Who should have coordinated the Confederate attacks?

*Teaching point 2:* Fire support. Where was the Confederate artillery? Was their absence a key factor in the Confederate failure? Was the Union artillery effective?

*Teaching point 3:* Battle command. Evaluate Bragg's performance. Was he doing his job on this part of the field? Was it a good idea for the Confederate commanders to divide the battlefield into sectors in the middle of a battle?

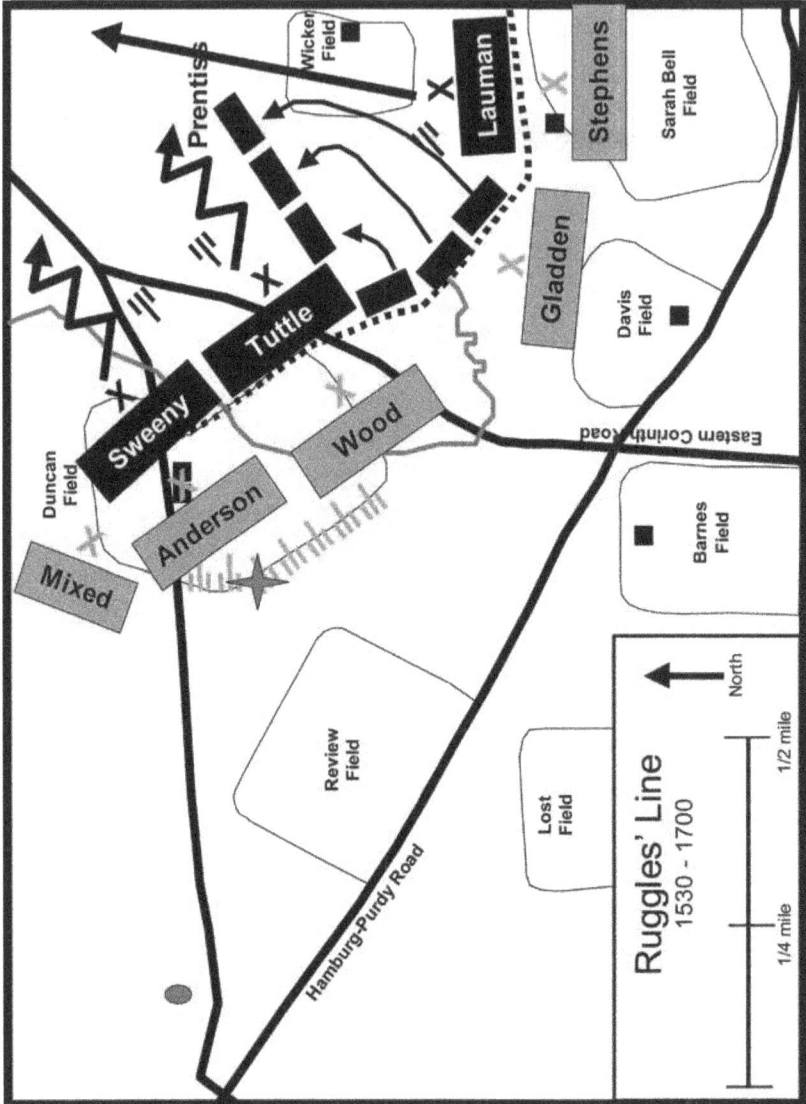

Wicker Field

Lauman

Stephens

Sarah Bell Field

Prentiss

Gladden

Davis Field

Tuttle

Sweeny

Duncan Field

Wood

Anderson

Mixed

Eastern Corinth Road

Barnes Field

Review Field

Lost Field

Hamburg-Purdy Road

**Ruggles' Line**
1530 - 1700

North

1/4 mile   1/2 mile

Map 20.

# Stand 13

## Ruggles' Line

*Directions:* Walk back north over the bridge. As soon as you cross the bridge, turn left (west) and cross Duncan Field. Move to the line of cannons. You are now along the Confederate artillery position known as Ruggles' Line. Today this line includes some of the most rare guns in the United States. The many different types of cannons also exemplify the lack of standardization of the Confederate artillery.

*Description:* Southeast of W.H.L. Wallace and Prentiss the Union line started to crumble. The numerous Confederate attacks had worn down the Federal defenders. By 1530 Hurlbut's troops had fallen back, exposing Prentiss' left flank. By 1600 Prentiss had bent his line back 90 degrees to refuse the flank.

Confederate leaders now realized that infantry alone would not carry the line along the Sunken Road. Beginning at 1530 Confederate officers started gathering all available artillery units on the field. The officer who orchestrated this concentration is not really known definitely. BG Ruggles later asserted he was responsible, while Hardee's Chief of Artillery Major Francis Shoup also claimed credit. Needless to say numerous officers were probably responsible for this concentration, which by 1630, numbered 53 cannons. This was possibly the largest artillery concentration in North America up to that time. While the Confederates formed this line, a considerable artillery duel began. For 1 hour the cannoneers traded fire, the Union gunners compelling a few Confederate artillery units to retire.

As more Confederate artillery units arrived and the Confederate bombardment reached its peak, the Union batteries on the ridge behind the Sunken Road now started to fall back. The Confederate artillery was setting the conditions for a successful attack. At 1630 a coordinated Confederate attack struck the defenders along the Sunken Road. Union units started to break. The first to go was Sweeny's brigade that was attacked frontally from across Duncan Field while additional Confederate units struck it from the north on its right flank. As Sweeny's men fell back, he rode to Wallace to tell him of the collapse. Wallace ordered the entire division to retire. Things were now very confused in the Union line; four of Wallace's regiments did not get the word to retire. Soon the Union line crumbled. Small units and individuals tried to withdraw as the Confederates closed around them. Prentiss found out that Wallace was pulling back, and at 1700 Prentiss also ordered a retreat.

*Vignette:* Captain C.P. Searle, 8th Iowa Infantry, in Sweeny's brigade, described the destruction in the Hornet's Nest: "The enemy, being encouraged by additional forces, made another frightful assault from three directions—front and flanks—pouring shot and shell into our ranks with fearful effect. Finally, with two hundred or more dead and wounded, and after ten hours of hard fighting, with very little cessation, seeing that we were surrounded, the order came to retire, but too late. We started from the high ground on which we had been fighting down a ravine, on the retreat, hoping to be able to cut through the Rebel lines, which were at our rear and had been for two hours. We started back under a most galling fire of grape and canister, seeming to come from every direction. An incident here may not be uninteresting. Retreating on the double quick, with leaden and iron hail flying thick around us, a soldier a pace in front of me fell, and I was so close that I fell over him. At the same time a spent ball struck my left arm and another went through my canteen. My arm tingled with pain, and the little water left in my canteen was warm and running over me as I feel to the ground. I thought it was my lifeblood. In fact, I was sure I was killed, but spying a 'Reb' close by, coming with all speed, for they had us on the run, I made one grand, desperate effort to gain my feet, and, much to my surprise, succeeded without trouble. I assure you I was a pretty lively corpse, for I left old 'Butternut' far in the rear, and did not even say 'Good day.' The poor fellow that I stumbled over was not so fortunate. He had received his final discharge." (C.P. Searle, "Personal Reminiscences of Shiloh," *Sketches and Incidents,* vol. I, Des Moines: Press of P.C. Kenyon, 1893, 333-34.)

*Teaching point 1:* Fire support. Was the Confederate artillery support the key to reducing the Union line? Who was responsible for ensuring the infantry had adequate artillery support?

*Teaching point 2:* Clarity of orders. Who was responsible for four regiments not getting the withdrawal order?

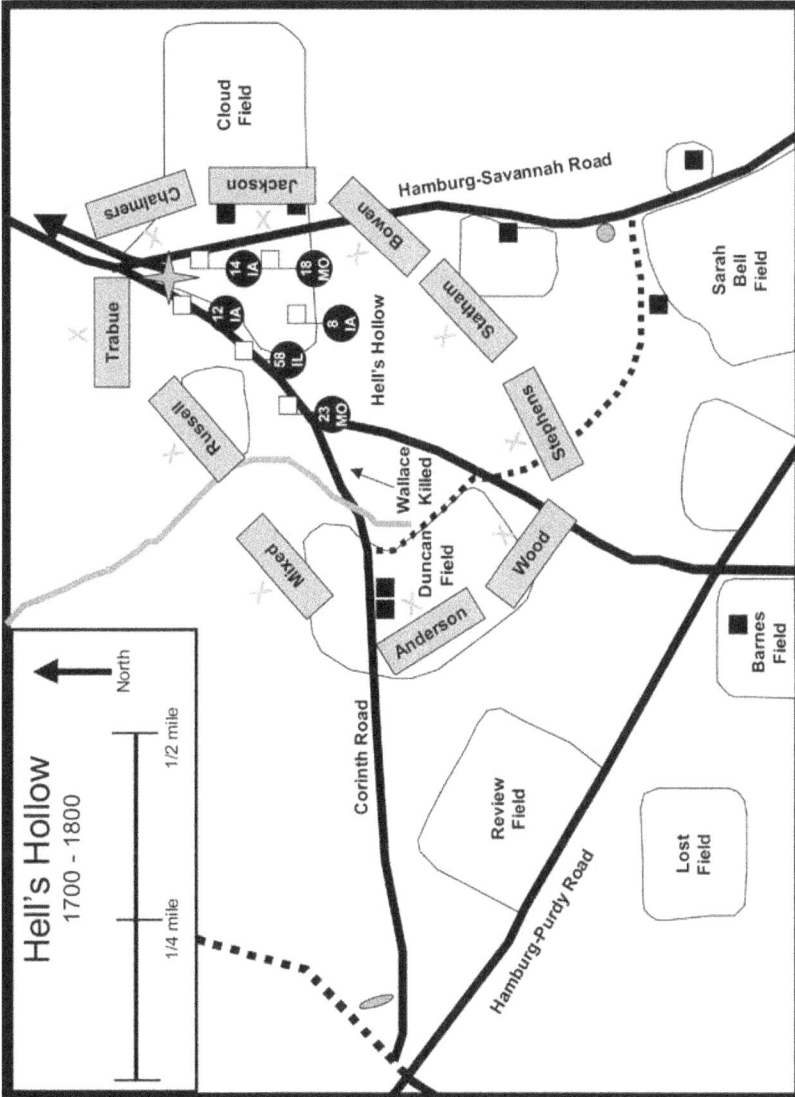

Hell's Hollow
1700 - 1800

North

1/4 mile    1/2 mile

Cloud Field

Chalmers

Jackson

Hamburg-Savannah Road

Bowen

Trabue

14 IA

18 MO

12 IA

Statham

8 IA

58 IL

Hell's Hollow

Russell

23 MO

Stephens

Wallace Killed

Mixed

Duncan Field

Anderson

Wood

Sarah Bell Field

Corinth Road

Review Field

Hamburg-Purdy Road

Lost Field

Barnes Field

Map 21.

109

# Stand 14

## Hell's Hollow

*Directions:* Walk back to your vehicle. Do a U-turn (if in a bus, you will have to drive down the road to find a place to turn around) and travel northeast on Corinth-Pittsburg Road for .4 mile. Pull over by the United Daughters of the Confederacy monument. Dismount and walk to the monument. Cloud Field is to your east, and Hell's Hollow is the low ground to the southwest.

*Description:* All along the Sunken Road line, Union troops were trying to escape as the Confederates encircled them. Artillerymen limbered up and made for Pittsburg Landing, driving their horses into a frenzy. The infantrymen were left to their own devices. Some units attempted to maintain their integrity while other units disintegrated into small bands.

By 1630 W.H.L. Wallace was trying to get his men out of the trap. Sitting on his horse, Wallace turned to get a better view when he fell hard to the ground. A bullet hit Wallace in the back of the head, exiting through his left eye. Initially Wallace's staff officers started to carry him to the rear, but they soon decided he was dead and fearing their own capture, they gently placed Wallace's body behind some ammunition boxes and ran away. Wallace was not dead, however. Counterattacking Union troops found Wallace on 7 April, and he was evacuated to Savannah. Wallace's wife, Ann, had arrived at Pittsburg Landing on the morning of 6 April for a surprise visit, and she now nursed her critically injured husband. Wallace lingered until 10 April and died in his wife's arms.

All around the fleeing Union troops, Confederate units "tightened the noose." Confederate units that had been fighting Sherman and McClernand now circled in from the west. Confederate units that had been fighting on the far Confederate right now came in from the east. Additional Confederate pressure came from units in the center that pressed the attack when they saw the Federals falter.

At 1730 large bands of Union troops started to surrender. The 14th Iowa and 18th Missouri were the first to be completely trapped, and they soon surrendered. A ravine ran behind the Sunken Road line, and many Union soldiers were captured there. The men came to know this ravine as "Hell's Hollow." The 23d Missouri, 58th Illinois, and 8th Iowa all surrendered there. The 12th Iowa made it a little farther north before it too joined the others in captivity. Battery B, 2d Michigan Light Artillery lost four cannon and had 56 men captured as Confederate cavalrymen chased them down before they could escape. Prentiss tried to escape, but at Hell's

Hollow he was forced to surrender his sword to COL William Rankin of the 9th Mississippi.

Despite the surrender, confusion reigned on this part of the field. Some Union troops surrendered, while a few hundred feet away other Federals continued to fight on. Seeing blue uniforms, some Confederates fired on the Union soldiers, not knowing they had surrendered. Some units armed with modern rifles attempted to destroy their weapons before their capture, and Confederates fired on them to prevent the loss. Two Confederate regiments swapped their antiquated weapons for modern Enfields captured from surrendering Union troops.

By 1800 it was over. In the end, approximately 2,200 Union soldiers were surrounded and compelled to surrender. The men along the Sunken Road line had withstood numerous charges by several Confederate brigades from 1000 to 1700. They had bought Grant valuable time to reorganize and prepare a new defensive line, time he used well.

*Vignette:* CPT Searle, who we left at Ruggle's Line, described his capture: "My time had come to receive personal attention. A big, burly Rebel captain stepped up to me and said, 'You d----d Yankee, give me your sword!' Oh, how I did want to give it to him point first. But discretion prevailed, and I gave it to him hilt first, which probably saved the burial squad two interments." (C.P. Searle, "Personal Reminiscences of Shiloh," *Sketches and Incidents*, vol. I, Des Moines: Press of P.C. Kenyon, 1893, 335.)

*Teaching point 1:* Timeliness of orders. Did the Union commanders wait too long to give the order to retreat?

*Teaching point 2:* Selfless service. Was the capture of the 2,000 Union soldiers necessary? Was their loss necessary, or were they sacrificed?

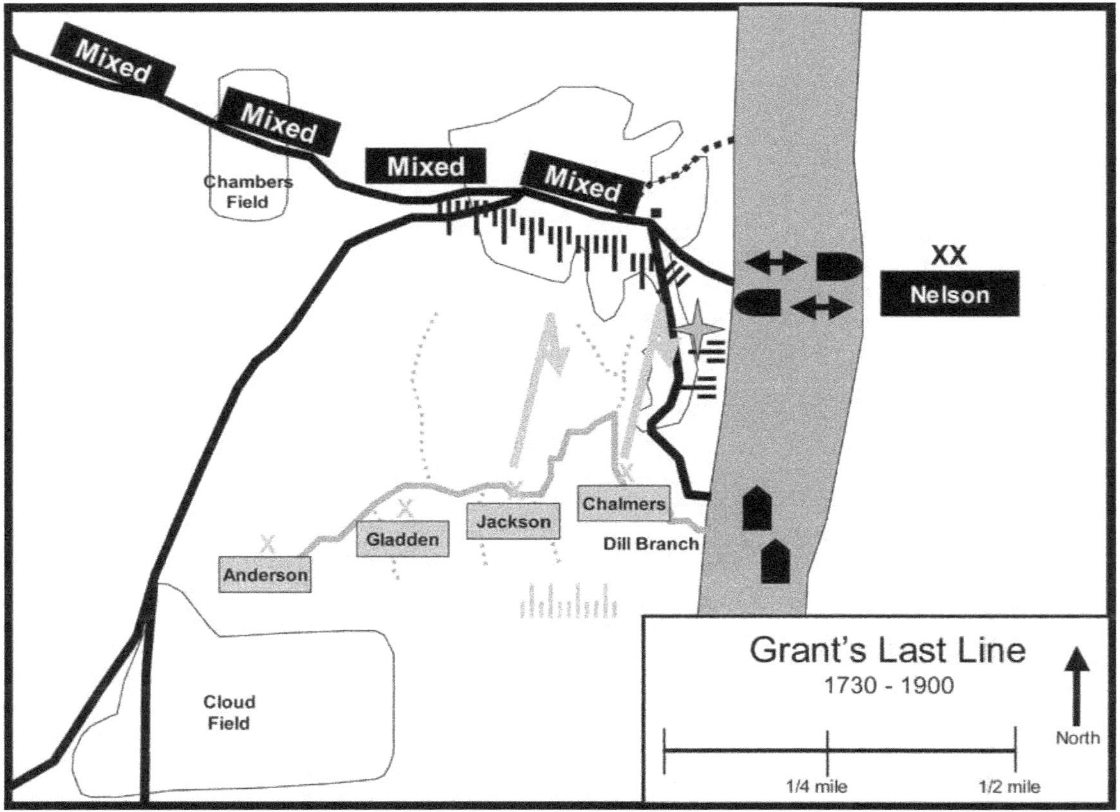
Mixed
Mixed
Mixed
Mixed
Chambers
Field
XX
Nelson
Chalmers
Jackson
Gladden
Anderson
Dill Branch
Cloud
Field
Grant's Last Line
1730 - 1900
North
1/4 mile
1/2 mile

Map 22.

## Stand 15

## Grant's Last Line

*Directions:* Go north on Corinth-Pittsburg Road for .8 mile. Turn right (east) on Pittsburg Landing Road (notice the long line of cannons). Park in the lot by the National Cemetery. Dismount and walk down Riverside Drive to the cannons and marker for Margraf's battery.

*Description:* At 1430 Grant told his chief of staff, COL Joseph D. Webster, to begin forming a last line of defense on the ridge south of Pittsburg Landing. Using the time Sherman and McClernand gained at Jones Field and W.H.L. Wallace and Prentiss along the Sunken Road, Webster laid out a formidable line. Initially he established the position with three unused batteries (including a battery of 24-pound siege guns). As artillery units fell back from the front, Webster arranged for their resupply and then placed them in line. By 1700 Webster had 52 cannons under his control.

When Grant departed Savannah that morning, he did not know that MG Don Carlos Buell had arrived there the day before. Before leaving for the battlefield, Grant ordered BG William "Bull" Nelson of Buell's army to move his division down the east side of the river to Pittsburg Landing. Grant had promised guides, but none ever arrived. Nelson lost 6 hours trying to find a passable route on the flooded east side, but his division moved at 1300. Buell, meanwhile, took a steamer to Pittsburg Landing where he met with Grant around 1300. The meeting was brief and revolved around moving Buell's troops to Pittsburg Landing.

At 1700 Nelson's lead brigade, commanded by COL Jacob Ammen, arrived across the river from Pittsburg Landing. Nelson arranged for boats in the river to start moving his men across, and by 1800 he had about 600 men west of the river and in line.

After reducing the pocket at the Hornet's Nest, Bragg believed that one more attack would destroy Grant's army. He placed artillery on a ridge south of Dill Branch and formed four brigades—Chalmers', Jackson's, Deas', and Anderson's—for an attack. All was ready by 1800 when Chalmers' and Jackson's brigades attacked. The men first had to cross the deep ravine of Dill Branch. As the men ascended the northern side, they met the fire of the gun line Webster had formed. Additionally, the gunboats *Tyler* and *Lexington* in the Tennessee River opposite the mouth of Dill Branch added large-caliber naval shells to the Federal defensive artillery barrage. Under such a concentrated bombardment, the Confederates did not stand long under this fire. As Chalmers and Jackson retreated, Bragg was surprised to see units to their left retiring. Beauregard had ordered a halt to the fighting for the day, directing his commanders to retire a short distance away.

At his headquarters at Shiloh Church, Beauregard received a telegram from Colonel Ben Helm saying that Buell's Army was near Decatur, Alabama, nowhere near the battlefield (Helm had seen one of Buell's divisions, not his whole army). He assessed his army to be exhausted and disorganized. He knew daylight was almost gone. Now armed with the incorrect information that Buell was far away, Beauregard ordered a halt to the fighting. He dispatched staff officers across the field with the message to end the day's action. Apparently, Beauregard planned to finish Grant in the morning. When Bragg learned of Beauregard's order, he was livid. As he considered what to do, he noticed troops falling back. Bragg exclaimed, "My God, my God, it is too late!"

*Vignette:* Sometimes the remembrance of an event depends on the echelon of command. This is a Confederate corps commander's perception of the gunboat fire: "They were covered by a battery of heavy guns, well served, and their two gunboats, which now poured a heavy fire upon our supposed positions, for we were entirely hid by the Forrest. Their fire, though terrific in sound and producing some consternation at first, did us no damage, as the shells passed over and exploded far beyond our positions." (General Braxton Bragg, *OR*, vol. 10, part 1, 466.)

A Confederate regimental commander had a different opinion of the gunboats: "I then flanked to the left about 300 yards and halted to rest, but in a very few minutes the shelling from the gunboats was so as to be unbearable, killing and wounding several of my men. I thereupon retired to a ravine and remained until dusk, and then moved back and encamped for the night." (Lieutenant Colonel C.D. Venable, 5th Tennessee, *OR*, vol. 10, part 1, 434.)

*Teaching point 1:* Culmination. With the information known to Beauregard, was the decision to stop fighting for the night the correct one?

*Teaching point 2:* Battle command. Was Beauregard in the correct location to make the decision to stop fighting? Should Beauregard have consulted with his corps commanders before halting the fight?

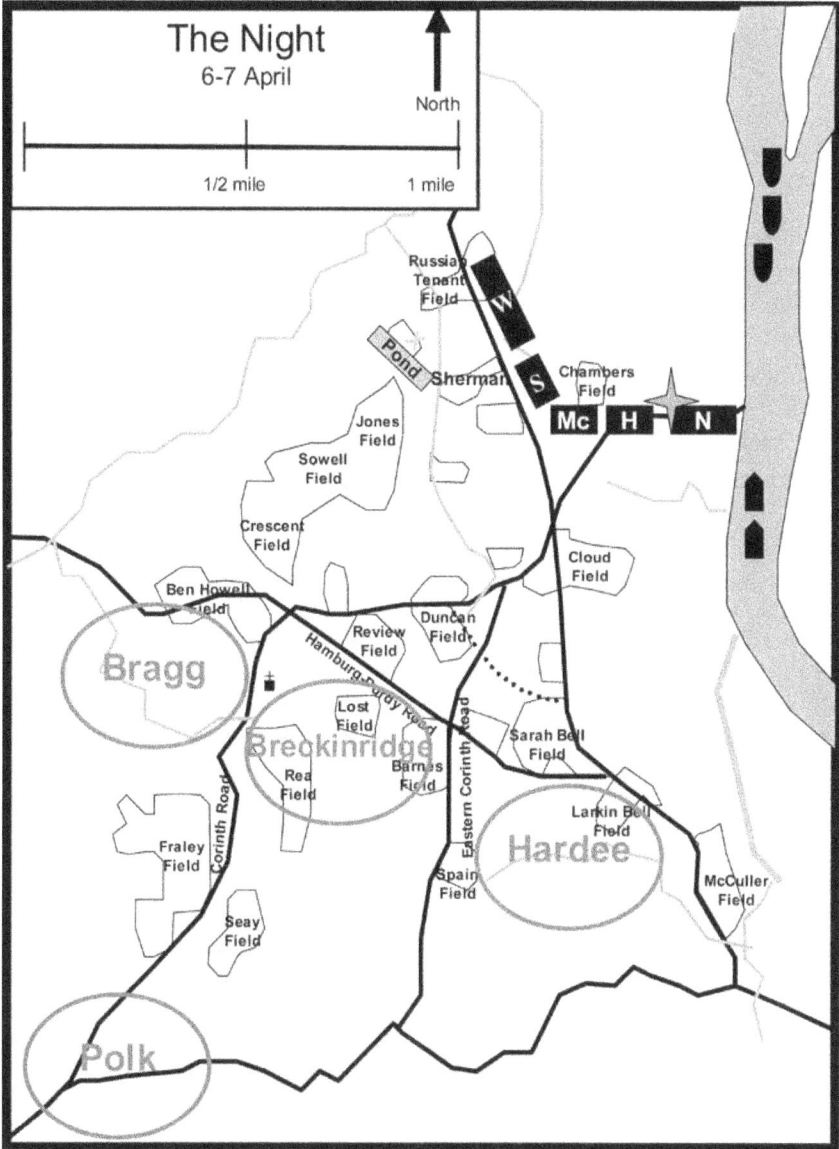

The Night
6-7 April

North

1/2 mile     1 mile

Russian Tenant Field

Pond

Sherman

W

S

Chambers Field

McH N

Jones Field

Sowell Field

Crescent Field

Cloud Field

Ben Howell Field

Review Field

Duncan Field

Bragg

Hamburg-Purdy Road

Lost Field

Sarah Bell Field

Breckinridge

Barnes Field

Rea Field

Eastern Corinth Road

Lankin Bell Field

Corinth Road

Hardee

Fraley Field

Spain Field

McCuller Field

Seay Field

Polk

Map 23.

115

# Stand 16

## The Night

*Directions:* Walk north on Riverside Drive toward your vehicle. Stop at the intersection where you can see the landing and Grant's line to the west.

*Description:* The Army of the Tennessee had been roughly handled on 6 April. It had lost most of its camps and had been driven back 2 miles. Its back was to the Tennessee River. One division commander had been mortally wounded and left on the field, and another had been captured. Numerous brigade and regiment commanders were on the casualty list. Near dark Lieutenant Colonel James McPherson joined Grant around a fire. McPherson asked Grant if he should prepare to retreat. Grant replied, "Retreat? No! I propose to attack at daylight and whip them." At 1915 Lew Wallace's division arrived on the field and joined Sherman. Grant now had 5,800 fresh troops. The Army of the Tennessee had been bent but not broken.

After the Confederate withdrawal, Nelson continued shuttling Army of the Ohio units across the river, completing the move at 2100. Nelson's troops saw quite a spectacle as they arrived at Pittsburg Landing. Up to 10,000 men of the Army of the Tennessee were cowering below the bluffs. Grant had been trying to get these men to rejoin their outfits, but they wanted no more fighting and disregarded him. These sulkers had been trying to get on any boat that landed, which hampered evacuating the wounded and resupplying the Army. As Nelson's troops landed, these survivors told tales of woe and warned the men. Nelson became irritated and shouted, "Damn your souls, if you won't fight, get out of the way, and let men come here who will!"

At 2100 the first troops of BG Thomas Crittenden's division of the Army of the Ohio arrived. Crittenden's men arrived on boats from Savannah. By 2300 all of Crittenden's men were ashore. Buell would continue moving his troops to Pittsburg Landing during the night; he would eventually have 18,000 men available on 7 April. When complete, the Union dispositions ran (from west to east): Lew Wallace's division, Sherman's division, McClernand's division, Hurlbut's division, Crittenden's division, and Nelson's division. Prentiss' division was effectively destroyed, and W.H.L. Wallace's division (under COL Tuttle) was behind the line trying to reorganize.

Buell and Grant had only one short meeting on 6 April, and they did not discuss operations for 7 April. Both men were army commanders and independent of each other. There was no overall commander on site on the Union side. However, both commanders had independently decided to attack.

At 2200 rain began to fall, and it came down in torrents. The Union soldiers had no tents or proper equipment, having lost it all when their camps were overrun. The men just had to lie in the rain, trying to get what sleep they could. Adding to the misery, the *Tyler* and *Lexington* fired shots all night long in the hope of preventing the Confederates from sleeping. They also prevented the Union troops from getting any sleep.

Beauregard spent the night in Sherman's tent by Shiloh Church. He met with each corps commander during the night. All of the Confederate commanders were ecstatic. They decided to rest the men and reorganize in the morning to complete the destruction of Grant's army. When the rains came at 2200, the Confederates occupied the Union camps. During the night Hardee's men camped south of Sarah Bell Field, Breckinridge in the center, Bragg in the west around Sherman's camps, and for unknown reasons, Polk camped at his bivouac site of 5 April, almost 2 miles from the field. Pond's brigade did not get the word, and it stayed in position in close proximity to the Union troops.

Not all of the Confederates retired to the captured tents. COL Nathan Bedford Forrest conducted a reconnaissance by dressing his men in captured blue overcoats. Forrest's men moved to where they could see the landing and were surprised to learn Buell's troops were arriving. Forrest found Hardee and passed along this intelligence bonanza. Hardee told him to go to Beauregard's headquarters, but Forrest could not find it. Forrest returned and ordered another reconnaissance, which again learned that more of Buell's troops were arriving. No one would take Forrest's report.

The Confederate commanders slept in captured tents that night thinking that only the routed Army of the Tennessee was to their front. They were convinced that Buell was far away. They were sure of victory in the morning. Forrest held the critical information but could not get it to the proper authorities.

*Vignette:* A private in Nelson's division described Pittsburg Landing: "At the landing—but how shall I attempt to set the picture forth? I have never yet seen told in print the half of the sickening story. Wagons, teams and led horses, quartermaster's stores of every description, bales of forage, caissons—all of the paraphernalia of a magnificently appointed army—were scattered in promiscuous disorder along the bluff side. Over and all about the fragmentary heaps, thousands of panic-stricken wretches swarmed from the river's edge far up toward the top of the steep; a mob in uniform, wherein all arms of the service and well-nigh every grade were commingled in utter confusion; a heaving, surging herd of humanity, smitten with a very frenzy of fright and despair, every sense of manly pride, of honor, and duty, completely paralyzed, and dead to every feeling save the most abject, pitiful terror. A number of officers could be distinguished amid the tumult, performing the pantomimic accompaniments of shouting incoherent commands, mingled with threats and entreaties. There was a little drummer boy, I remember too, standing in his shirt sleeves, pounding his drum furiously, although to what purpose we could not divine. Men were there in every stage of partial uniform and equipment; many were hatless and coatless, and but few retained their muskets and their accouterments complete. Some stood wringing their hands, and rendering the air with cries and lamentations, while others, in the dumb agony of fear, cowered behind the object that was nearest them in the direction of the enemy, though but the crouching form of a comrade. . . . There was a rush for the boat when we neared the landing, and some, wading out breast deep into the stream, were kept off only at the point of a bayonet." Anonymous Private, 6th Ohio, Nelson's division. (Ebenezer Hannaford, *The Story of a Regiment: A History of the Campaigns and Associations in the Field of the Sixth Regiment, Ohio Volunteer Infantry,* Cincinnati, 1868, 567.)

*Teaching point 1:* Reorganization and consolidation. The Confederate soldiers had fought hard all day and were exhausted. With the information known at the time, should the Confederate commanders have reorganized that night or let the men rest?

*Teaching point 2:* Perseverance. Grant had been defeated on 6 April. He had the means to evacuate his troops. Should he have withdrawn his battered army?

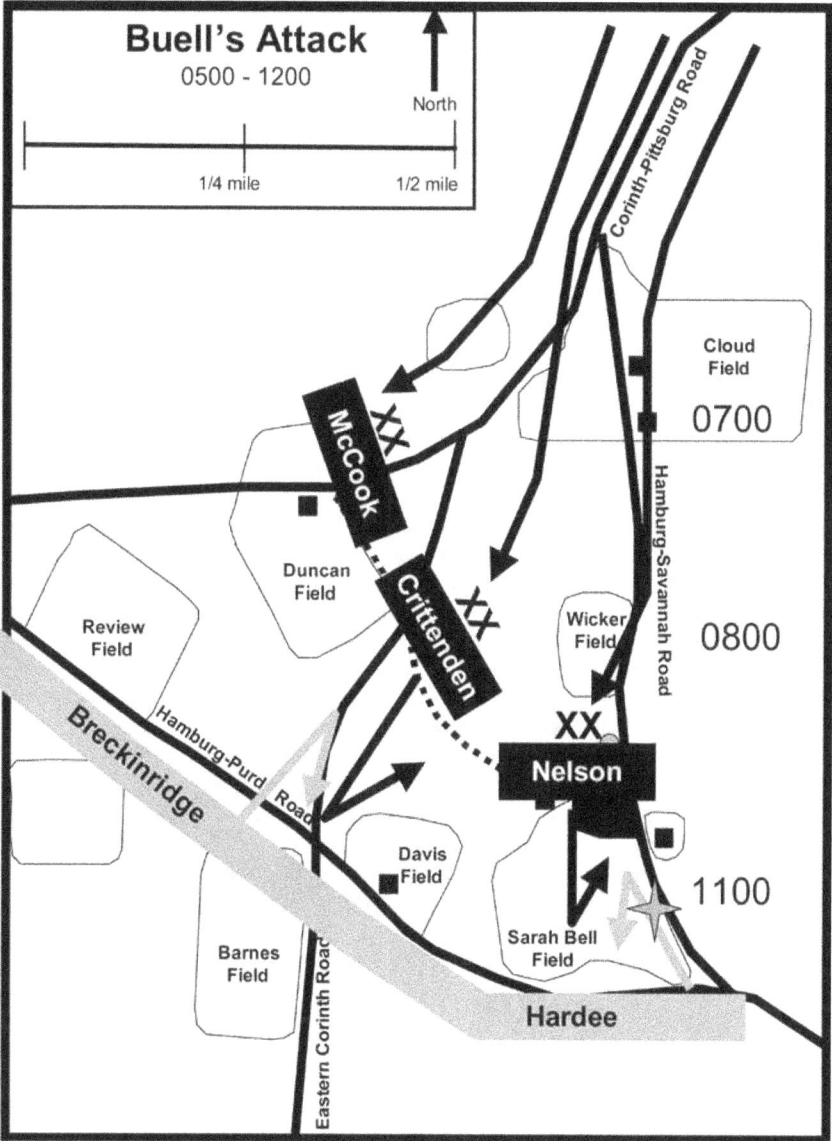

Map 24.

119

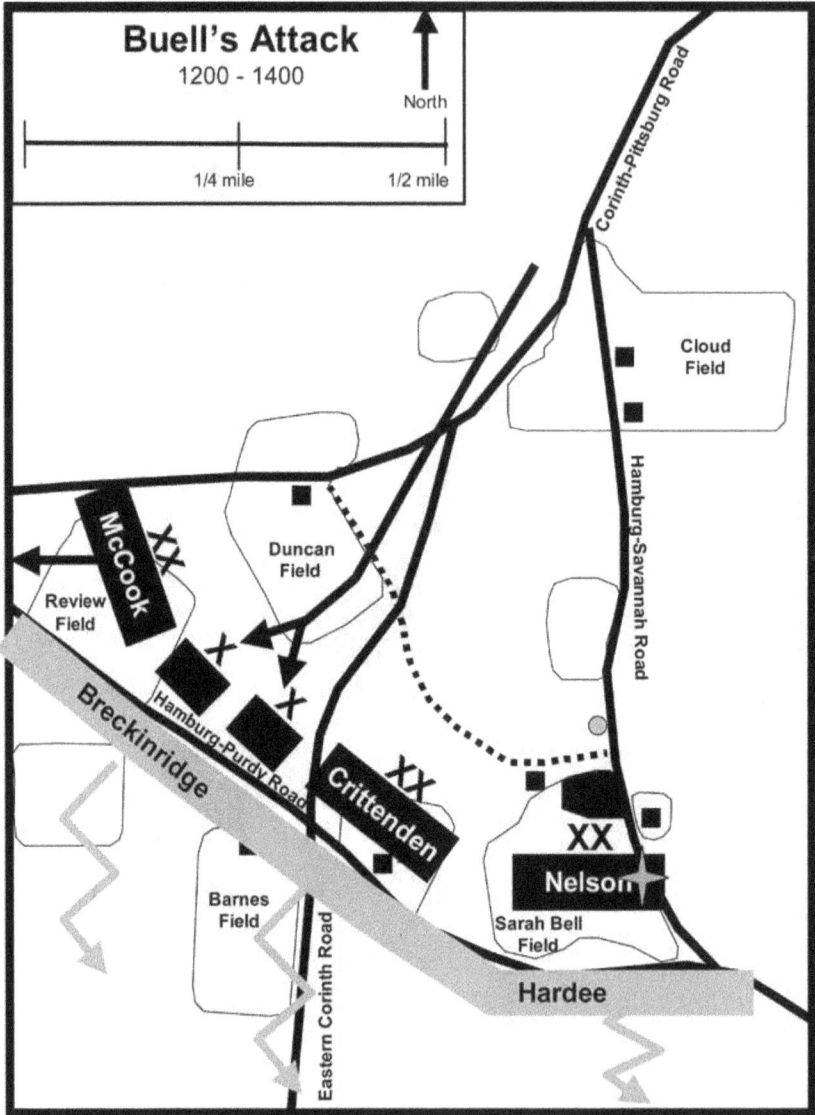

## Buell's Attack
### 1200 - 1400

North

1/4 mile  1/2 mile

Corinth-Pittsburg Road

Cloud Field

Hamburg-Savannah Road

McCook

Duncan Field

Review Field

Breckinridge

Hamburg-Purdy Road

Crittenden

Barnes Field

Eastern Corinth Road

Sarah Bell Field

Nelson

Hardee

Map 25.

120

# Stand 17

## Buell's Attack

*Directions:* Travel west on Pittsburg Landing Road. Turn left (south) on Corinth-Pittsburg Landing Road for .8 mile. Turn left (south) on Hamburg-Savannah Road for .8 mile. Pull into the parking lot north of the peach orchard. Dismount and move to the field.

*Description:* At 0500 on 7 April, Buell's attack started with the advance of Nelson's division. Nelson had all three of his brigades on the line and slowly advanced south against almost no opposition. By 0700 Nelson had reached Cloud Field and halted while BG Thomas Crittenden's two brigades formed on his right. With two divisions now on the line the attack continued south. Soon the Union troops encountered Confederate pickets who fired and quickly fell back. Nelson's troops entered Wicker Field and began to receive artillery and concentrated infantry fire. For 90 minutes Nelson's men fought a long-range battle with Confederate troops in Sarah Bell Field. Nelson had not brought his artillery with him, so Buell assigned one of Crittenden's batteries to him. While fighting in Wicker Field, BG Lovell Rousseau's brigade from BG Alexander McCook's division arrived from the landing and joined the line on Crittenden's right. At 1000 the Union line resumed the advance. Nelson's division moved to the north end of Sarah Bell Field and Crittenden to the Sunken Road.

Hardee was surprised that his pickets in Cloud and Wicker Fields had been pushed back. He was expecting an easy morning, but now Union troops were pushing hard against his position. Hardee threw any brigade he could find into the line to stem the Union attacks. By 1100 Nelson and Crittenden attacked south from the Sunken Road and from the peach orchard in Sarah Bell Field. COL Sanders Bruce's brigade and COL Ammen's brigade from Nelson's division assaulted all the way to Davis Field, capturing a Confederate battery. Several Confederate regiments were thrown in to stem this penetration. The battle seesawed back and forth, but eventually, the Union troops withdrew to positions along the Sunken Road.

Hardee, seeing the Union troops retreating, ordered a counterattack. A makeshift brigade made of remnants led the attack. Having been told that friendly troops were to the front, this ad hoc unit did not cover his line with skirmishers. As they entered Sarah Bell Field, Moore's men were decimated when Ammen's brigade opened fire. Seeing Moore's difficulties, Hardee sent a mixture of the other units to attack Nelson. (Confederate organizational structure had disintegrated by this time, even at brigade level. Commanders organized demi-brigades from available regiments, gave them a commander, and sent them forward.) The combatants traded fire for a while, but by 1200 the Confederates had withdrawn from Sarah Bell Field and Nelson had pulled back to Wicker Field.

To the west in Crittenden's area, the fighting also seesawed. COL Robert Trabue's brigade of Confederates attacked COL Morgan Smith's brigade of Federals but was repulsed. Crittenden's division followed Trabue all the way to the Hamburg-Purdy Road, but Confederate artillery forced it back to Duncan Field.

By this time, McCook's entire division had arrived and was now in line on Crittenden's right. Bragg commanded this part of the field for Beauregard and ordered Russell's brigade to attack the Federals. Russell was easily repulsed, and McCook pursued him. McCook's troops made it to Review Field before counterattacks and artillery forced them back. During this fight, Kentucky Governor George W. Johnson, serving as a private in the Confederate 4th Kentucky, was mortally wounded.

A little after 1200 Buell's troops attacked again. Until 1400 Buell's troops fought hard to gain ground. On the left Nelson's men made steady progress and by 1400 had reached the Hamburg-Purdy Road. Crittenden pressed down Eastern Corinth Road until he, too, reached Hamburg-Purdy Road. On the right McCook advanced to the west along the Corinth-Pittsburg Landing Road. McCook's western movement opened a gap between himself and Crittenden, which was filled by brigades from Grant's army that had been in reserve. The disorganized, battle-weary Confederate army had held up the 18,000 fresh troops of Buell for 6 hours, but now the tide was turning.

*Vignette:* Captain F.A. Shoup, Hardee's chief of artillery, described the confusion on the Confederate side: "The commands were all mixed up. We were simply blown into line by the enemy's fire. I wanted to find General Hardee. I made my way to Shiloh Church, where I found Beauregard with an enormous staff. Just as I arrived, Pickett, Hardee's Adjutant, rode up with a message to the Commanding General. He had a hard time trying to make the General understand where Hardee was. It was astonishing how well we fought, and how well we held them, considering the horrible state of case with us the second day, and the new troops they had." (F.A. Shoup, "How We Went to Shiloh," *Confederate Veteran*, vol. 2, 1894, 140-41.)

*Teaching point 1:* Reorganization and consolidation. If the Confederates had reorganized during the night, could they have defeated Buell?

*Teaching point 2:* Battle command. Should Hardee have committed units as he found them, or should he have taken the time to organize units for attacks?

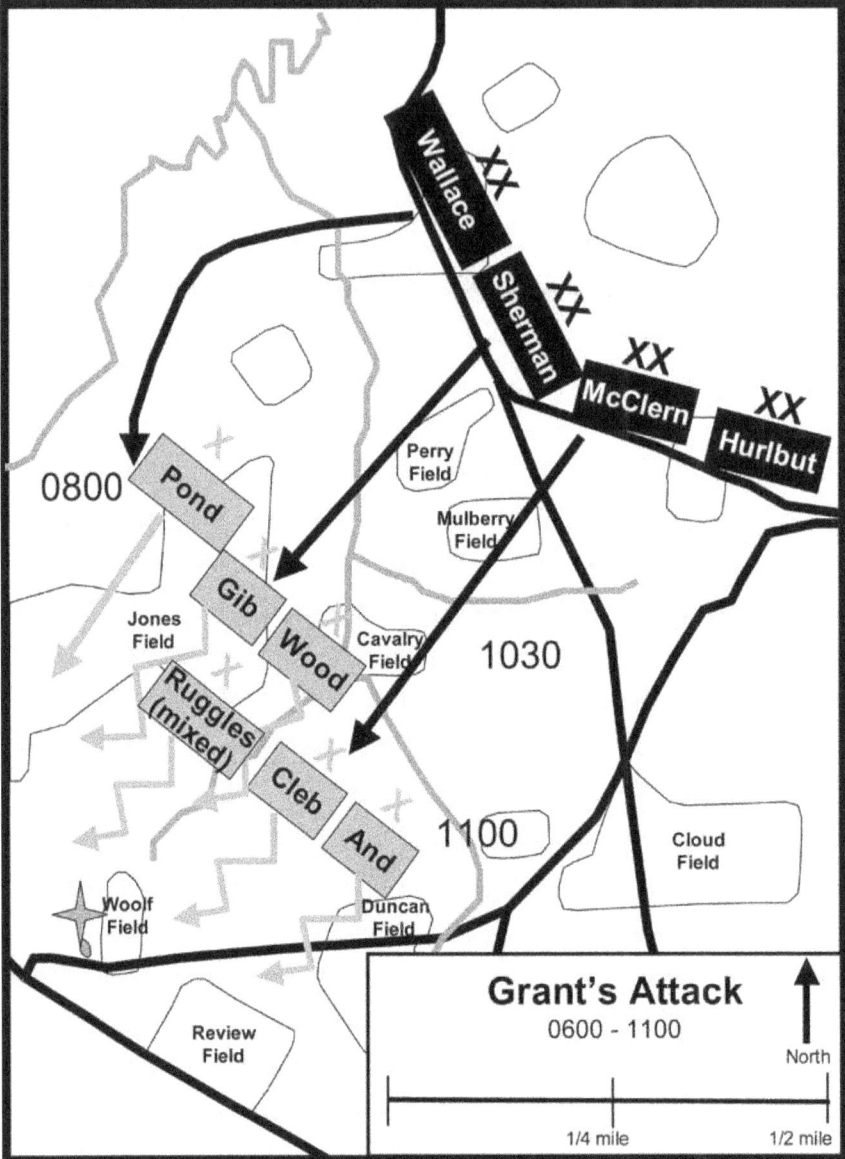

Map 26.

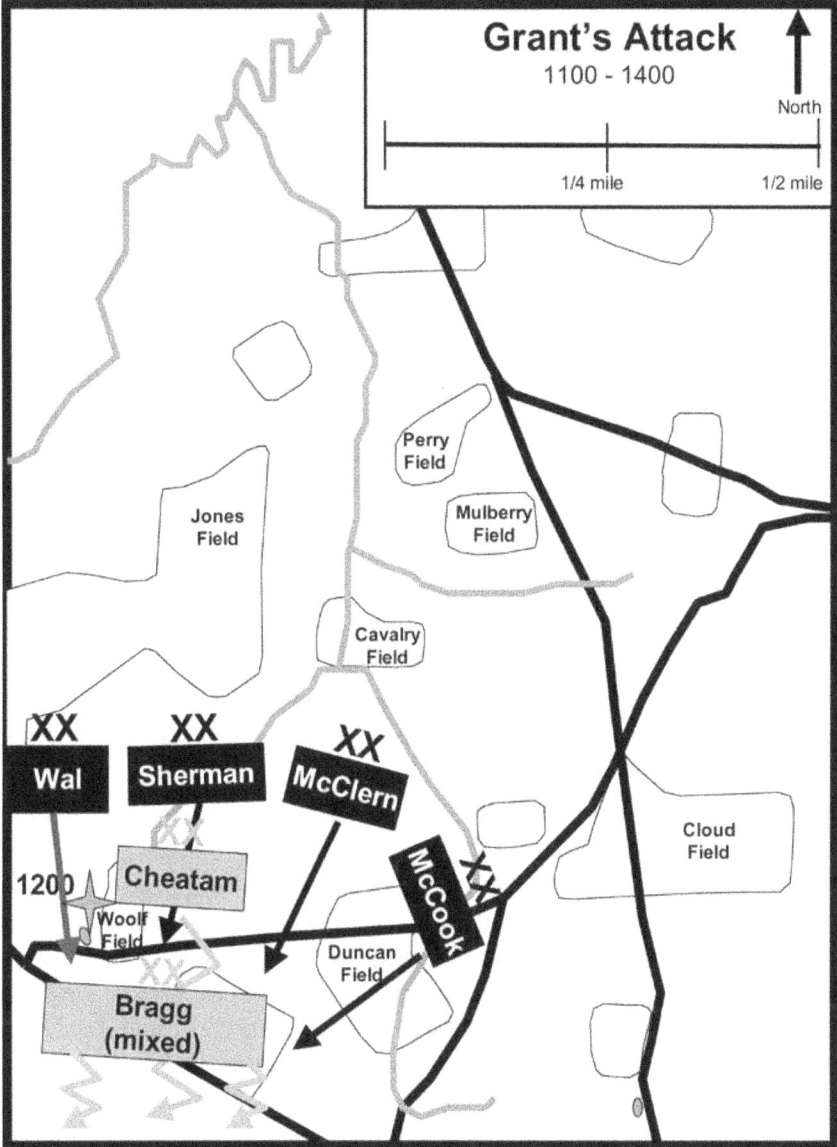

Map 27.

# Stand 18

## Grant's Attack

*Directions:* Go south on Hamburg-Savannah Road for .1 mile. Turn right (west) on Hamburg-Purdy Road for .7 mile. Turn right (north) on Eastern Corinth Road for .6 mile. Turn left (west) on Corinth-Pittsburg Landing Road for .7 mile. Park by Water Oak Pond. Dismount and move to the pond.

*Description:* As the sun came up on 7 April, three batteries of artillery assigned to Lew Wallace's division saw a Confederate battery in Jones Field, and they opened fire on them. Grant came to investigate and after observing a few minutes ordered Wallace to attack.

For some reason, COL Preston Pond had not withdawn during the night, and his tired Confederate troops faced Wallace's fresh division. Pond's battle-weary troops did not stand long, and Beauregard ordered them to the rear as a reserve. Wallace's troops retook Jones Field. In response to this threat, Gibson's and Wood's brigades were ordered to attack. This attack was initially successful, but Sherman brought his battered division on line and pushed the Confederates back. While Gibson and Wood were attacking, other Confederate units were forming a defensive line south of Jones Field. BG Daniel Ruggles gathered a group of unit fragments and Cleburne's and Anderson's brigades, all badly pounded the previous day.

The rest of Grant's troops arrived. McClernand formed on Sherman's left, and Hurlbut formed on McClernand's left. At 1030 Grant's army moved forward en masse. In a desperate effort to respond, Bragg ordered Cleburne to attack, an order he protested. Yet Cleburne attacked and his brigade was destroyed. The Confederate line was now untenable, and its units slowly began to give ground. Cheatham's division had spent the night well south of the field but had moved north early that morning. Hearing of the Union thrust, Cheatham advanced and ran into Sherman and McClernand. Cheatham stopped the Federal divisions, and when Wallace saw this, he ordered his division into the defense despite having no enemy to his front. Cheatham traded fire with the Union troops but eventually was forced back. While Cheatham was fighting, Bragg had formed another defensive line by Water Oaks Pond. Wallace, Sherman, and McClernand now advanced against this line and a 2-hour fight resulted. During this fighting, Beauregard was all over this part of the field, personally leading units into the fight.

At 1330 McCook's division advanced from Duncan Field and slammed into the flank of Bragg's line. Bragg, pressured on the front by Wallace,

Sherman, and McClernand and on the flank by McCook started to fall back south of the Hamburg-Purdy Road. Beauregard formed a small counterattack force built around Wood's brigade. These men splashed across Water Oaks Pond and pushed back McCook's men. McCook repositioned his troops and forced Wood back across Water Oaks Pond.

Beauregard now had only one unit left, Pond's brigade. Since withdrawing from Jones Field, Pond had been out of the fighting but stayed busy. Ruggles had ordered him to the far left. As he was moving, he was ordered to the far right to support Hardee. Before he could get there, Beauregard ordered him to the center in reserve. As he was complying, Polk ordered him to support his line. As he moved to Polk, Pond received an order from Beauregard to report to him. Beauregard personally led Pond's brigade, which slammed into the advancing Union troops and had momentarily stopped the Federal attack, but he was soon forced back. The Union troops crossed the Hamburg-Purdy Road at 1430.

With the Confederate line on the verge of collapse, a staff officer asked Beauregard, "General, do you not think our troops in the condition of a lump of sugar thoroughly soaked with water, but yet preserving its original shape, though ready to dissolve?" Beauregard replied, "I intend to withdraw in a few moments." True to his word, Beauregard sent staff officers around the field ordering the army back to Corinth. The Confederates tried to bring off as much of the spoils as possible when they retreated south. Beauregard formed a final line south of Shiloh Church to cover the withdrawal. By 1700 the Confederates had abandoned the field. Due to the late hour and the army's condition, the Union troops did not pursue that day.

*Vignette:* The fighting on this part of the field was very confused. Private Henry Stanley, 6th Arkansas, who we last saw at Fraley Field on 6 April recounted: "However, as despite our firing, the blues were coming uncomfortably near, I rose from my hollow; but, to my speechless amazement, I found myself a solitary grey, in a line of blue skirmishers! My companions had retreated! The next I heard was, 'Down with that gun Secesh, or I'll drill a hole through you! Drop it quick!' Half a dozen of the enemy were covering me at that same instant, and I dropped the weapon, incontinently. Two men sprang at my collar, and marched me, unresisting, into the ranks of the terrible Yankees. *I was a prisoner*!" (Henry M. Stanley, *The Autobiography of Sir Henry Morton Stanley*, Cambridge, MA: Riverside Press, 1909, 200.)

*Teaching point 1:* Culmination. Was Beauregard correct in ordering a retreat? Was the Army of the Mississippi defeated?

*Teaching point 2:* Pursuit. Should the Union have pursued the Confederates in a timely manner? Was the Federal victory complete?

# Stand 19

## The Cost

*Directions:* Walk north on McClernand Road; the road will veer to the northwest. Halt at the Confederate burial trench at the apex of the curve in the road.

*Description:* On the morning of 8 April Sherman, with two infantry brigades and two squadrons of cavalry slowly, pursued the Confederates south. At Fallen Timbers, Sherman ran into a small cavalry force under COL Nathan Bedford Forrest's command. When Forrest saw the lead Union regiment forming, he charged. Forrest's charge broke up the Union troops, but while withdrawing, Forrest was shot in the hip at point blank range. Legend has it that Forrest scooped up a Union infantryman and used him as a shield as he rode away, dropping him when he was out of danger. Sherman was convinced the Confederates were gone and returned to the vicinity of Pittsburg Landing. The Battle of Shiloh was over.

The Union troops held the field, and collecting the dead and wounded became the first priority. More than 8,000 Union and 1,000 Confederate wounded were on the battlefield. Additionally, more than 3,500 Union and Confederate dead had to be buried. The Union troops buried their own dead first, some in long trenches and others in individual graves. In 1866 the Union dead were disinterred and moved to the National Cemetery on the bluff overlooking the landing. The Confederate dead were also buried in trenches, but the Union burial parties were not as careful with the Confederate dead. The Confederates were stacked on top of each other in the trenches (legend says seven deep). Today, five of these trenches have been located on the field.

The battle was costly. More Americans fell at Shiloh than the total casualties in all of the previous wars United States had fought. Exact numbers are difficult to determine, but according to the official records, the casualties follow:

|  | Killed | Wounded | Missing | Total |
|---|---|---|---|---|
| Army of the Tennessee | 1,513 | 6,601 | 2,830 | 10,944 |
| Army of the Ohio | 241 | 1,807 | 55 | 2,103 |
| Union Totals | 1,754 | 8,408 | 2,885 | 13,047 |
| Army of the Mississippi | 1,728 | 8,012 | 959 | 10,699 |
| Total | 3,482 | 16,420 | 3,844 | 23,746 |

*Vignette:* Wilbur F. Crummer, 45th Illinois, a Union soldier on a burial detail described the process: "On Tuesday I was detailed with others to bury the dead lying within our camp and a distance of two hundred yards in advance. I had charge of digging the grave, if a trench over sixty feet long and four feet deep, can be called a grave. The weather was hot, and most of the dead had been killed early Sunday morning, and dissolution had already commenced. The soldiers gathered up the bodies and placed them in wagons, hauling them near to the trench, and piling them up like cord wood. We were furnished with plenty of whiskey, and the boys believed it would have been impossible to have performed the job without it. When the grave was ready, we placed the bodies therein, two deep; the father, brother, husband and lover, all to lie till Gabriel's trumpet shall sound. All the monument reared to those brave men was a board, nailed to a tree at the head of the trench, upon which I cut with my pocket knife, the words: '125 rebels.' We buried our Union boys in a separate trench, and on another board were these words: '35 Union.' " (Wilbur F. Crummer, *With Grant at Fort Donelson, Shiloh, and Vicksburg,* Oak Park, IL: E.C. Crummer & Co., 1915, 74-75.)

*Teaching point 1:* Graves registration. How can commanders best deal with the dead on a battlefield?

*Teaching point 2:* The cost of battle. How do you prepare soldiers for the carnage of a battlefield? How do you minimize the psychological effects of death on soldiers?

## Stand 20

## The War is Won

*Directions:* Return to your vehicle. Go west on Hamburg-Purdy Road for .5 mile. Turn right (north) on TN 22 for 1.7 miles. Turn right (east) on Pittsburg Landing Road for .9 mile. Park near the National Cemetery and walk through the cemetery to the monument of three large cannons. You are at the location of Grant's headquarters.

*Description:* The campaign leading up to the battle and the battle of Shiloh itself had been hard on Ulysses S. Grant. He had been removed from command, and his superior seemed to lack confidence in him. On 6 April his army nearly had been destroyed and had suffered thousands of casualties. His original headquarters was a small building on the bluff, but surgeons had taken over the building. Where once he controlled the battle, now the cabin was filled with piles of amputated limbs and the screams of the wounded. Thousands of his soldiers had run from the battlefield and were now cowering under the bluffs. Throughout the day numerous subordinates had either asked Grant if he was going to retreat or had recommended that he do so. Grant would have none of it. He was here to stay.

Arguably, Grant's determination was one of the keys to victory for the Union during the American Civil War. In 1863 Grant spent seven months reducing the garrison at Vicksburg. He tried numerous ways to accomplish the mission, and when they each failed in turn, he developed a new plan until one worked. His forward movement after the Battle of the Wilderness in 1864 surprised many on both sides; they were all accustomed to Army of the Potomac commanders retreating after losing a battle. Grant did not retreat; he kept the pressure on the armies of the Confederacy and forced them to quit. Grant truly first demonstrated his determination to win at Shiloh.

During the rainstorm on the night of 6 April, Grant rested under a tree at this location. Despite the severe setback of the day Grant was resolved to attack in the morning. He would not let the misfortunes of 6 April affect him. Grant was resolved to win the Battle of Shiloh, and he did. He would demonstrate the same determination to win throughout the Civil War, and in the end, he was victorious.

*Vignette:* After the fighting had ended on 6 April, Sherman went to Grant's headquarters to talk to him about retreating across the Tennessee River: "I started out to find Grant and see how we were to get across the river. It was pouring rain and pitch dark, there was considerable confusion, and the only thing just then possible, as it seemed to me, was to put the river between us and the enemy and recuperate. Full of only this idea, I ploughed around in the mud until at last I found him standing backed up against a wet tree, his hat well slouched down and coat well pulled up around his ears, an old tin lantern in his hand, the rain pelting on us both, and the inevitable cigar glowing between his teeth, having retired, evidently, for the night. Some wise and sudden instinct impelled me to a more cautious and less impulsive proposition than at first intended, and I opened up with, 'Well, Grant, we've had the devil's own day, haven't we?' 'Yes,' he said, with a short, sharp puff of the cigar: 'lick 'em tomorrow though.'" (William T. Sherman, *Washington Post*, in "Grant's Pertinacity," *Army and Navy Journal*, 30 December 1893, 317.)

## IV. Integration Phase for the Battle of Shiloh

As defined in *The Staff Ride* by Dr. William G. Robertson, a staff ride consists of three phases. The first phase is the Preliminary Study Phase. This phase is conducted before the visit to the battlefield and prepares students for the visit. It may take various forms, including classroom instruction, individual study, or a combination of the two. The second phase is the Field Study Phase. This phase is conducted on the battlefield and better allows students to understand historical events through analyzing the actual terrain. The third phase is the Integration Phase. No staff ride is complete without the Integration Phase because it is critical for students to understand what happened, why it happened, and most important, what can be learned by studying the battle. The staff ride leader can conduct the Integration Phase on the battlefield immediately after completing the Field Study Phase. However, it is recommended that, when possible, students have some time for personal reflection and thought. Thus the Integration Phase may best be conducted the day after the Field Study Phase ends.

The staff ride leader can organize the Integration Phase based on the unit, time available, and training objectives. The leader can conduct the Integration Phase like an after-action review or may simply lead a discussion with students on what they learned. The following are potential Integration Phase topics the staff ride leader could use.

**Synchronization.** Throughout the battle, both sides had difficulty coordinating their units to mass maximum combat power at a decisive point. Recall the piecemeal Confederate attacks at Rea Field, Sarah Bell Field, and the Hornet's Nest. Discuss how a modern officer or soldier can learn the value of synchronization from studying this battle.

**Mass.** During the Battle of Shiloh, commanders were unsuccessful until they massed their available combat power at a decisive point. The Confederates attacked into Rea Field for 2 hours with more troops than the Union defenders, but they were unsuccessful until they were able to mass their available units all at once. The same is true at Sarah Bell Field. Discuss the benefits of mass to a modern officer or soldier using lessons from Shiloh.

**Battle command.** The staff ride leader can discuss how certain commanders exercised command in operations against a hostile, thinking enemy. There are a plethora of examples during this battle. Discuss Johnston as a commander and a leader. Discuss how certain commanders were able to be successful despite the odds while others failed miserably. Discuss Grant's actions throughout the battle; was he critical to the victory? Discuss the location of command posts in view of their suitability for the task.

**Fire support.** The staff ride leader can discuss the success and failure of fire support throughout the battle. Discuss artillery command and control. Discuss the successes of fire support (Ruggles' Line, Grant's Last Line) and its failure (Hornet's Nest, Jones Field).

**Planning and orders.** The staff ride leader can discuss the effects of planning and order dissemination. Discuss the Confederate plan: was it a good plan, were the formations the best possible, was it executed as drafted, was it flexible and adaptable, how did they branch from the original plan? Discuss orders and order dissemination. Discuss the problem between Grant and Lew Wallace. Discuss Beauregard ending the fighting on 6 April.

**Intelligence and reconnaissance.** The staff ride leader can discuss how intelligence affected the battle. Discuss what each side knew about the other and how it affected the battle. Discuss the role of cavalry and other reconnaissance troops. Discuss Forrest's reconnaissance on the night of 6 April.

**Face of battle.** Some things do not change on any battlefield—death, destruction, maiming, and carnage. How did the soldiers and leaders react to the ghastly scenes at Bloody Pond and along the Sunken Road?

These are just a few examples the staff ride leader can use during the Integration Phase. Ask students what they learned of lasting value and scrutinize each issue to gain the most benefit for a modern officer or soldier.

# V. Support for a Staff Ride to Shiloh

1.  Information and assistance.

    a.   The Staff Ride Team, Combat Studies Institute (CSI), Fort Leavenworth, Kansas, has conducted Shiloh staff rides for military groups and can provide advice and assistance on every aspect of the battle. The Staff Ride Team can also provide staff ride leadership for a Shiloh staff ride. Visit the CSI web site for information on obtaining staff ride leadership. Additional support includes battle information, detailed knowledge of the battle and battlefield, and familiarity with the Shiloh battlefield and surrounding areas.

    Address:    U.S. Army Command and General Staff College
                Combat Studies Institute
                ATTN: ATZL-SWI
                Fort Leavenworth, KS 66027-6900

    Telephone:  DSN 552-2078
                Commercial (913) 684-2078

    Web site:   http://cgsc.leavenworth.army.mil/csi/staff_ride/

    b.   The National Park Service, which maintains the Shiloh National Military Park, can provide advice and assistance to any group desiring to visit the park. The Visitors Center includes a small museum with a film on the battle, a bookstore, and restrooms. There is a small fee to enter the park, but military groups can be exempted. Coordinate group plans with the park headquarters before your visit.

    Address:    Superintendent
                Shiloh National Military Military Park
                1055 Pittsburg Landing Road
                Shiloh, TN 38376

    Telephone:  (731) 689-5275

    Web site:   http://www.nps.gov/shil/

2.  Logistics.

    a.   Meals. No facilities exist within the park, but a few restaurants are within a 5-minute drive of the park. The nearest fast-food restaurants are located in Savannah, Tennessee, approximately 12 miles from the park. There is one picnic area located within the park's boundary. Groups may consider bringing food and drinks with them on the staff ride and eating meals in the picnic area to save time.

    b.   Lodging. The nearest quality lodging is in Savannah, which has several national chain motels. Additionally, Savannah has a campground. Corinth, Mississippi, is approximately 20 miles from the battlefield but is a bigger city with a Civil War museum, hotels, and restaurants. Pickwick Landing State Park is 40 minutes from Shiloh and has camping, a lodge, cabins, and a restaurant.

    c.   Medical. The Park Rangers are trained in first aid and can call for aerial evacuation. The nearest hospital is the Hardin County General Hospital in Savannah, approximately 15 minutes from the park. The phone number is (731) 926-8000.

3.   Other considerations.

    a.   Make provisions for liquids and food since they are not available on the battlefield. Personnel on the ride should carry water with them.

    b.   Ensure the group has proper clothing. The battlefield is rural, so good hiking boots and outdoor clothing are required. Be prepared for inclement weather since violent thunderstorms can occur in any season.

    c.   Environmental hazards include ticks, snakes (water moccasins in the wet areas and copperheads throughout), and poison ivy. Check weather conditions and forecasts before traveling to the battlefield.

    d.   Maintain good relations with the Shiloh National Military Park. Coordinate with them well in advance, and ascertain current road conditions, construction, etc. Follow the park rules.

# Appendix A

## Order of Battle, Union Forces

Numbers in parentheses: present/killed/wounded/missing
K = killed, MW = mortally wounded, W = wounded, C = captured

### The Army of the Tennessee
MG Ulysses S. Grant

### 1st Division
MG John A. McClernand

1st Brigade, COL A.M. Hare (W), COL M.M. Crocker (2,214/104/467/9)
    (8 IL, 18 IL, 11 IA, 13 IA, D/2 IL)
2d Brigade, COL C.C. Marsh (1,847/80/475/30)
    (11 IL, 20 IL, 45 IL, 48 IL)
3d Brigade, COL J. Raith (MW), LTC E.P. Wood (2,153/96/393/46)
    (17 IL, 29 IL, 43 IL, 49 IL, Carmichael's cavalry)
Not brigaded troops (727/5/35/0)
    (Cavalry: Stewart's regiment  Artillery: D/1 IL, E/2 IL, 14 OH battery)

### 2d Division
BG W.H.L. Wallace (MW)
COL James Tuttle

1st Brigade, COL J. Tuttle (1,804/39/143/676)
    (2 IA, 7 IA, 12 IA, 14 IA)
2d Brigade, BG J. McArthur (W), COL T. Morton (2,548/99/470/11)
    (9 IL, 12 IL, 81 OH, 13 MO, 14 MO)
3d Brigade, COL T. Sweeny (W), COL S. Baldwin (3,571/127/501/619)
    (8 IA, 7 IL, 50 IL, 52 IL, 57 IL, 58 IL)
Not brigaded troops (485/5/58/0)
    (Cavalry: C/2 US Cav, I/4 US Cav, A&B/2 IL Cav  Artillery: A/1 IL,
D/1 MO, H/1 MO, K/1 MO)

### 3d Division
MG Lewis Wallace

1st Brigade, COL M. Smith (1,998/18/114/0)
    (8 MO, 11 IN, 24 IN)
2d Brigade, COL J. Thayer (2,236/20/99/3)
    (1 NE, 22 IN, 58 OH, 68 OH)
3d Brigade, COL C. Whittlesey (2,541/2/32/1)
    (20 OH, 56 OH, 76 OH, 78 OH)

Not brigaded troops (789/1/5/0)
    (Cavalry: 3/5 OH Cav, 3/11 IL Cav  Artillery: L/1 MO, 9 IN Battery)

## 4th Division
### BG Stephen A. Hurlbut

1st Brigade, COL N. Williams (2,407/112/532/43)
    (3 IA, 28 IL, 32 IL, 41 IL)
2d Brigade, COL J. Veach (2,722/130/492/8)
    (25 IN, 14 IL, 15 IL, 46 IL)
3d Brigade, BG J. Lauman (1,751/70/384/4)
    (31 IN, 44 IN, 17 KY, 25 KY)
Not brigaded troops (945/5/33/56)
    (Cavalry: 1&2/5 OH Cav  Artillery: 13 OH Battery, Mann's battery, 2 MI Battery)

## 5th Division
### BG William T. Sherman

1st Brigade, COL J. McDowell (1,903/137/444/70)
    (6 IA, 46 OH, 40 IL, 6 IN Battery)
2d Brigade, COL D. Stuart (W), COL T. Smith (1,939/80/380/90)
    (55 IL, 54 OH, 71 OH)
3d Brigade, COL J. Hildebrand (1,883/70/221/65)
    (53 OH, 57 OH, 77 OH)
4th Brigade, COL R. Buckland (2,107/36/203/74)
    (48 OH, 70 OH, 72 OH)
Not brigaded troops (771/2/28/0)
    (Cavalry: 1&2/4 IL Cav  Artillery: B/1 IL, E/1 IL)

## 6th Division
### BG B.M. Prentiss (C)

1st Brigade, COL Peabody (K) (2,790/113/372/236)
    (21 MO, 25 MO, 16 WI, 12 MI)
2d Brigade, COL M. Miller (C) (2,509/44/228/178)
    (18 MO, 61 IL, 18 IA)
Not brigaded troops (889/78/328/16)
    (Infantry: 18 WI, 23 MO, 15 IA  Cavalry: 11 IL Cav  Artillery: 5 OH Btry, 1 MN Btry)

Unassigned troops of the Army of the Tennessee (2,031/39/159/17)
    (Infantry: 15 MI, 14 WI. Artillery: 8 OH Btry, H/1 IL, L/1 IL, B/2 IL F/2 IL)

## The Army of the Ohio
MG Don Carlos Buell

### 2d Division
BG Alexander McCook

4th Brigade, BG L. Rousseau (3,207/28/280/3)
    (1 BN/15 US, 1 BN/16 US, 1 BN/19 US, 1 OH, 6 IN, 5 KY)
5th Brigade, COL E. Kirk (W) (2,721/34/310/2)
    (77 PA, 29 IN, 30 IN, 34 IL)
6th Brigade, COL W. Gibson (3,074/25/220/2)
    (15 OH, 49 OH, 32 IN, 39 IN)
H/5th US Battery (116/1/13/0)

### 4th Division
BG William Nelson

10th Brigade, COL J. Ammen (1,876/16/106/8)
    (6 OH, 24 OH, 36 IN)
19th Brigade, COL W. Hazen (1,761/48/357/1)
    (6 KY, 9 IN, 41 OH)
22d Brigade, COL S. Bruce (1,898/93/603/20)
    (1 KY, 2 KY, 20 KY)
2 IN Cav (87/0/2/0)

### 5th Division
BG Thomas L. Crittenden

11th Brigade, BG J. Boyle (2,179/33/212/18)
    (19 OH, 59 OH, 9 KY, 13 KY)
14th Brigade, COL W. Smith (Unk/25/157/10)
    (13 OH, 11 KY, 26 KY)
Not brigaded troops (246/2/6/0)
    (Cavalry: 3 KY Cav  Artillery: G/1 OH, H&M/4 US)

### 6th Division
BG T.J. Wood

20th Brigade, BG J. Garfield (not engaged)
    (64 OH, 65 OH, 13 MI, 51 IN)
21st Brigade, COL G. Wagner (1,723/0/4/0)
    (15 IN, 40 IN, 57 IN, 24 KY)

# Appendix B

## Order of Battle, Confederate Forces

Numbers in parentheses: killed/wounded/missing
K = killed, MW = mortally wounded, W = wounded, C = captured

### The Army of the Mississippi
General Albert S. Johnston (K)
General Pierre G.T. Beauregard

### I Corps
MG Leonidas Polk

1st Division—4,988 men
BG Charles Clark

    1st Brigade, COL R. Russell (97/512/0)
        (11 LA, 12 TN, 13 TN, 22 TN, Bankhead's battery)
    2d Brigade, BG A. Stewart (93/421/3)
        (14 AR, 4 TN, 5 TN, 33 TN, Stanford's battery)

2d Division—3,032 men
BG Benjamin F. Cheatham

    1st Brigade, BG Bushrod Johnson (120/607/13)
        (Blythe's MS, 2 TN, 15 TN, 154 TN, Polk's battery)
    2d Brigade, COL W. Stephens (75/413/3)
        (7 KY, 1 TN, 6 TN, 9 TN, Smith's battery)
    Cavalry (0/0/0)
        (1 MS, Brewer's AL&MS)

### II Corps
MG Braxton Bragg

1st Division—7,672 men
BG Daniel Ruggles

    1st Brigade, COL R. Gibson (97/488/97)
        (1 AR, 4 LA, 13 LA, 19 LA, Bain's battery)
    2d Brigade, BG P. Anderson (69/313/52)
        (1 FL BN, 17 LA, 20 LA, 9 TX, Confederate Guards Response Battalion, 5 Co/Washington Artillery)
    3d Brigade, COL P. Pond (89/336/169)
        (16 LA, 18 LA, Crescent Regiment, Orleans Guard Battalion, 38 TN, Ketchem's battery)
    Jenkin's Cavalry Bn (2/5/1)

2d Division—7,783 men
BG Jones M. Withers

1st Brigade, BG A. Gladden (129/597/103)
(21 AL, 22 AL, 25 AL, 26 AL, 1 LA, Robertson's battery)
2d Brigade, BG J. Chalmers (83/343/19)
(5 MS, 7 MS, 9 MS, 10 MS, 52 TN, Gage's battery)
3d Brigade, BG J. Jackson (86/364/194)
(17 AL, 18 AL, 19 AL, 2 TX, Girardey's battery)
1st AL Cav (0/0/0)

## III Corps
MG William J. Hardee

1st Brigade, 2,360 men, BG T. Hindman (109/546/38)
(2 AR, 6 AR, 7 AR, 3 Confederate, Swett's battery, Miller's battery)
2d Brigade, 2,789 men, BG P. Cleburne (188/790/65)
(2 TN, 15 AR, 6 MS, 5 TN, 23 TN, 24 TN, Shoup's artillery battalion, Watson's battery)
3d Brigade, 2,508 men, BG S. Wood (107/600/38)
(7 AL, 16 AL, 8 AR, 9 AR Battalion, 3 MS Battalion, 27 TN, 44 TN, 55 TN, Harper's battery)

## Reserve Corps
BG John C. Breckinridge

1st Brigade, 2,691 men, COL P. Traubue (151/557/92)
(4 AL Battalion, 31 AL, 15 AR, 3 KY, 4 KY, 5 KY, Crew's artillery battalion, Byrne's battery, Cobb's battery, Morgan's cavalry)
2d Brigade, 1,744 men, BG J. Bowen (98/498/28)
(9 AR, 10 AR, 2 Confederate, 1 MO, Hudson's battery)
3d Brigade, 3,079 men, COL W. Statham (137/627/45)
(15 MS, 22 MS, 19 TN, 20 TN, 28 TN, 45 TN, Forrest's cavalry, Rutledge's battery)

# Appendix C. Biographical Sketches

## Union Commanders

**Ulysses S. Grant.** Grant was born on 27 April 1822 at Point Pleasant, Ohio, given the name Hiram Ulysses Grant (Ulysses Simpson came from an administrative error while enrolling at ther US Military Academy, West Point, New York). He entered West Point in 1839 but was not a good student, graduating 21 of 39 in the class of 1843. Grant joined the infantry and served in the Mexican War where he served in the 4th Infantry Regiment. He participated in the campaigns of Zachary Taylor and Winfield Scott and earned two brevets for valor. After the war Grant served in the Pacific Northwest where he quickly became bored and started to drink. Such problems caused Grant to resign his commission in 1854.

From 1854 to 1861 Grant tried his hand at farming, real estate, local politics, and store clerking. When the Civil War broke out, Grant obtained command of the 21st Illinois Infantry Regiment, receiving the rank of colonel. As Grant readied his regiment for combat, he was commissioned a brigadier general on 7 August 1861, in large part because of his connections with Illinois Representative Elihu B. Washburne. This relationship would benefit Grant throughout the war. Grant's first major combat came when he led the army component of the joint force that seized Fort Henry and Fort Donelson. These victories brought Grant to the favorable attention of the US public. Yet Grant's career faltered after he was surprised and almost defeated at the Battle of Shiloh. Grant was replaced as commander of the Army of the Tennessee until MG Henry Halleck, commander of the western Union forces, was selected to be the General in Chief of the Army and moved to Washington. Grant again assumed command of the Army of the Tennessee and spent December 1862-July 1863 attacking Vicksburg. When he finally succeeded in besieging and capturing that city, he virtually guaranteed control of the Mississippi River for the Union. After MG William Rosecrans' Army of the Cumberland was defeated at Chickamauga and besieged in Chattanooga, Grant led the relief forces and raised the siege.

Grant's triumphs impressed President Lincoln, and he was promoted to Lieutenant General and selected to be General in Chief of the Army. Grant devised a plan that called for all Union armies to attack the Confederacy simultaneously in 1864. Grant's determination in 1864 and 1865 ensured success for the Union, and Grant accepted the surrender of the Army of Northern Virginia on 9 April 1865. As a national hero, Grant was easily elected President of the United States in 1868. Unfortunately, his two terms as President were filled with corruption and scandal. Grant died in 1885. His memoirs remain a classic of military literature.

**William T. Sherman**. Sherman was born at Lancaster, Ohio, on 8 February 1820. His father died when Sherman was nine, and young William was sent to live with Senator Thomas Ewing (Sherman later married Ewing's daughter). Senator Ewing appointed Sherman to West Point, where he graduated in 1840, sixth in his class. Sherman spent an uneventful career before the war with Mexico where he earned one brevet. He resigned his commission in 1853 to pursue a banking career in California. When the bank failed, Sherman moved to Leavenworth, Kansas, and opened a law firm with two of his brothers-in-law. The law firm failed, so Sherman accepted the position as superintendent of the Louisiana State Seminary of Learning Military Academy (now Louisiana State University).

When Louisiana seceded from the Union, Sherman resigned and moved to St. Louis. Soon he was commissioned the colonel of the newly formed 13th US Infantry. Sherman was quickly appointed a brigadier general and commanded a brigade at First Bull Run. Sherman was then sent to command in Kentucky but was soon relieved by Don Carlos Buell for being unstable, having possibly suffered a nervous breakdown. After a period of rest, Sherman took command of a newly formed division under Grant, which he commanded at Shiloh. Promoted to major general in May 1862, Sherman was a corps commander under Grant during the Vicksburg Campaign. The Grant-Sherman relationship, initiated before Shiloh, was cemented at Vicksburg. Sherman moved with Grant to Chattanooga and fought on Missionary Ridge. When Grant was promoted to general in chief, Sherman assumed command of all troops in the west.

After seizing Atlanta, Georgia, in September 1864, Sherman left MG George Thomas' command to deal with the Confederate forces and led the rest of his army and marched toward Savannah, Georgia, leaving a swath of destruction along the way. Once Savannah fell, Sherman and his troops marched north toward Virginia. He accepted the surrender of Joseph Johnston's command near Durham Station, North Carolina, two weeks after General Robert E. Lee's surrender. When Grant was elected president, Sherman was appointed general in chief and promoted to general. Retiring from the Army in 1884, he spent his retirement years avoiding the numerous people who pestered him to run for president. Sherman died in 1891.

**John A. McClernand**. McClernand was born in Hardinsburg, Kentucky, on 30 May 1812. His family moved to Illinois when he was young and he was raised there. He was mainly self-educated, culminating with him passing the bar in 1832. McClernand soon entered politics and also served as a private in the Black Hawk War. When the Civil War started, President Lincoln commissioned him as a brigadier general of volunteers. McClernand used his position to further his political career, a stance that caused friction with Grant. He commanded a division at Shiloh and a corps at Vicksburg. Grant lacked confidence in him at both battles and relieved him of command during Vicksburg for "leaking" information to the press. After sitting out one year, McClernand was again appointed corps commander, this time in Louisiana. He resigned from the Army in late 1864. After the war McClernand returned to politics in Illinois where he died in 1890.

**William Harvey Lamb Wallace**. W.H.L. Wallace was born in Urbana, Ohio, on 8 July 1821. His family soon moved to Illinois where Wallace grew up and was admitted to the bar. He enlisted in an Illinois regiment during the Mexican War and eventually earned a commission. After the war, Wallace returned to practice law and entered politics. Soon after the outbreak of the Civil War, Wallace became colonel of the 11th Illinois Infantry. He commanded a brigade during the Fort Henry and Fort Donelson Campaigns and there earned brigadier general's stars. At Shiloh Wallace was leading his men in the Hornet's Nest when he was mortally wounded. Evacuated from the field, Wallace died at Savannah on 10 April 1862.

**Lewis Wallace**. Lew Wallace was born on 10 April 1827 at Brookville, Indiana. His father was governor of the state when Wallace was young. Wallace was a lieutenant in a volunteer regiment during the Mexican War. After the war he became a lawyer and was elected to the state senate in 1856. At the start of the Civil War, Wallace was placed in command of the 11th Indiana Infantry Regiment. Wallace and the regiment moved to the Eastern theater, but when he was promoted to brigadier general, he was returned to the west where he led a brigade during the Fort Henry and Fort Donelson Campaigns.

Promoted to major general and given command of a division, Wallace missed the first day of the Battle of Shiloh, something that tarnished him forever. He served out the rest of the war in minor posts, performing admirably in defending Washington in 1864. After the war Wallace was appointed to the military commission that tried the Lincoln conspirators and was president of the court-martial that convicted and condemned Henry Wirz, commander, Andersonville Prison. After leaving the Army Wallace failed to gain elective office, but he received political appointments. A prolific fiction writer after the war, he authored the famous novel *Ben-Hur*. Wallace died in 1905.

**Stephen A. Hurlbut**. Hurlbut was born in Charleston, South Carolina, on 29 November 1815. The son of a northern-born minister, Hurlbut spent his youth in the South. He joined the South Carolina Bar and served with a volunteer regiment during the Seminole War. In 1845 he moved to Illinois and entered politics, serving in the state legislature. At the outbreak of the Civil War he was commissioned brigadier general of volunteers, quickly rising to major general. He led a division at Shiloh and during the Corinth Campaign. He commanded a corps after Corinth and eventually commanded the Department of the Gulf. While in command of the Gulf area, he was accused of inappropriate efforts to gain personal profit, but he was allowed to leave the Army honorably in 1865. After the war he reentered politics, serving as minister to Colombia under Grant, and was eventually elected to the US House of Representatives. As minister to Peru, he again fell under the shadow of corruption. He died there in 1882.

**Benjamin M. Prentiss**. Prentiss was born in Belleville, Virginia (now West Virginia), on 23 November 1819. Prentiss spent his youth in Virginia but moved to Missouri with his family when he was 17. He eventually settled in Illinois, served in the militia, and commanded a company of volunteers during the Mexican War. After that conflict, he entered the bar and tried his hand at politics. At the outbreak of the Civil War, Prentiss was commissioned colonel of the 10th Illinois Infantry Regiment. He was soon promoted to brigadier general and given command of a division under Grant. During the Battle of Shiloh he was captured after holding the Hornet's Nest for 6 hours. Prentiss spent six months as a prisoner before he was finally exchanged. A participant in the court-martial of Fitz John Porter, Prentiss was promoted to major general but held only minor commands until he resigned his commission in October 1863. Prentiss returned to his law practice until President Grant gave him a political appointment as a pension agent. He died on 8 February 1901.

**Don Carlos Buell**. Buell was born on 23 March 1818 in Lowell, Ohio. He spent his youth in Indiana until he entered West Point, graduating in 1841, 32 of 52. Buell joined the 3d Infantry and served with it in Florida on the frontier and during the Mexican War. Buell was severely wounded during the war and earned two brevets. After the Mexican War he transferred to the adjutant general's department and held staff appointments on the frontier.

The start of the Civil War found Buell in California. He was promoted to brigadier general, and after arriving in Washington, he helped train the new Army of the Potomac. Next Buell was sent to Kentucky to lead troops to seize east Tennessee. Buell arrived on the second day of the Battle of

Shiloh, and his troops helped the Union win the victory. After the Corinth Campaign, Buell returned to Tennessee. When the Confederates invaded Kentucky in 1862, Buell followed and turned back the invasion by not losing the Battle of Perryville. The Confederates withdrew from Kentucky, but when Buell did not pursue, he was relieved of command. Buell waited a year for orders, but when none came, he resigned. After the war Buell ran an ironworks and coal mine in Kentucky. He died on 19 November 1898.

**William Nelson**. Nelson was born in Maysville, Kentucky, on 27 September 1824. Trained as a naval officer he was appointed midshipman in 1840 and served with the squadron that supported Winfield Scott during the Mexican War. Nelson was a Navy lieutenant when the Civil War started. President Lincoln commissioned him an Army brigadier general so he could use his state ties to raise troops in Kentucky. Nelson soon received command of a division under Buell, and his troops were the first reinforcements to reach the Shiloh battlefield. After the Corinth Campaign, Nelson was placed in command of troops in Kentucky where he was badly defeated at Richmond during the Confederate invasion. A month after this defeat Nelson was shot to death by fellow Union General Jefferson C. Davis who believed Nelson had insulted him.

# Confederate Commanders

**Albert Sidney Johnston.** Johnston was born in Washington, Kentucky, on 2 February 1803. He graduated from West Point in 1826. While at West Point Johnston became friendly with Jefferson Davis, the future president of the Confederate States of America. Johnston spent eight years in the Army and fought in the Black Hawk War. In 1836 he joined the Texas Army as a private and eventually rose to brigadier general. He served as Secretary of War for the Republic of Texas from 1838 to 1840. When Texas joined the United States, Johnston rejoined the US Army and in 1855 was commander, 2d Cavalry. In 1857 he led the famous expedition against the Mormons for which he earned promotion to brigadier general.

At the outbreak of the Civil War Johnston was commander, Department of the Pacific. He resigned his commission and after a laborious journey from California was appointed a full general in the Confederate Army in command of all troops in the west. Criticism of Johnston was severe after the Confederates in his command failed early in the war, but Davis, his old friend from West Point, had complete confidence in him. Johnston concentrated all available troops at Corinth in hope of striking a blow against Grant before Grant's and Buell's troops consolidated. In the resulting Battle of Shiloh Johnston was in the forefront of the fight until he was shot in the back of the knee. The bullet severed an artery, and Johnston died from loss of blood before a surgeon could be found.

**Pierre Gustave Toutant Beauregard.** P.G.T. Beauregard was born on 28 May 1818 in St. Bernard Parish, Louisiana. He graduated second in his class at West Point in 1838 and entered the engineers. During the Mexican War he served on Winfield Scott's staff and earned two brevets. Beauregard resigned his commission in early 1861 after he was relieved as Superintendent of West Point. He was appointed a brigadier general of the newly formed Confederate Army and placed in command of the Charleston, South Carolina, defenses. There he supervised the reduction of Fort Sumter. Beauregard served with distinction at the First Battle of Manassas under Joseph Johnston. He was promoted to general in July 1861 and sent to the west.

Although second in command to Albert Sidney Johnston at the Battle of Shiloh, he played a key role in planning the battle. After Johnston's death, Beauregard assumed command and withdrew the Army to Corinth. Ultimately Beauregard was forced to abandon Corinth, and while on sick leave, he was relieved of command. Beauregard was subsequently assigned to command the defenses of the Georgia and South Carolina coasts.

In June 1864 he joined Lee at Petersburg, and at the close of the war he was with Joseph Johnston again in North Carolina. After the war Beauregard was the president of a railroad. He died on 20 February 1893.

**Leonidas Polk**. Polk was born in Raleigh, North Carolina, on 10 April 1806. He entered West Point and graduated in 1827. While at West Point he became acquainted with Jefferson Davis. Six months after graduation Polk resigned his commission and entered the Episcopal ministry. He eventually rose to Missionary Bishop of the Southwest and founded the University of the South. At the outbreak of the war he was commissioned a major general in the Confederate Army and served in the west. When Albert Sidney Johnston concentrated forces for the Battle of Shiloh, Polk received command of a corps. Polk continued as a corps commander and fought at Shiloh, Perryville, Murfreesboro, and Chickamauga. On 14 June 1864, during the Atlanta Campaign, Polk was conducting a reconnaissance at Pine Mountain, Georgia, when a Federal artillery shell hit and instantly killed him.

**Braxton Bragg.** Bragg was born on 22 March 1817 at Warrenton, North Carolina. He graduated from West Point in 1837 and saw combat against the Seminole Indians and during the Mexican War. He was a lieutenant colonel when he resigned his commission in 1856 to become a plantation owner in Louisiana. Bragg was appointed a brigadier general of the Confederate Army early in the Civil War and commanded the district responsible for defending the coast from Pensacola to Mobile. Bragg brought 10,000 troops to Corinth and took command of a corps for the Battle of Shiloh. After Shiloh he was promoted to general and replaced Beauregard as commander of the renamed Army of the Tennessee.

Bragg invaded Kentucky in late 1862 but was forced to withdraw after the Battle of Perryville. Bragg defeated William Rosecrans at the Battle of Chickamauga, but a poor command climate crippled his army. After his defeat at Chattanooga and the subsequent withdrawal through Georgia, Bragg asked to be relieved of command. He next became the military adviser to President Jefferson Davis. At war's end he was serving under Joseph Johnston in North Carolina. After the war Bragg lived in Alabama and Texas until his death on 27 September 1876.

**William J. Hardee**. Hardee was born in Camden County, Georgia, on 12 October 1815. Hardee graduated from West Point in 1838 and served in the Mexican War where he was twice breveted for bravery. After the war he was the commandant of cadets at West Point and wrote *Rifle and Light Infantry Tactics*, the doctrinal manual both sides would use at the beginning of the Civil War. Hardee was commissioned a brigadier general in the new Confederate Army and organized troops in Arkansas. During the concentration at Corinth before the Battle of Shiloh, Hardee received command of a corps. After Shiloh Hardee continued as a commander in the Army of the Tennessee, seeing action at Perryville, Stones River, and Chattanooga. In 1864 Hardee asked to leave the Army of the Tennessee because he lacked confidence in the newly appointed commander, John Bell Hood. Hardee attempted to defend Savannah from Sherman, and at war's end he was also with Joseph Johnston in North Carolina. After the war Hardee was a planter. He died on 6 November 1873.

**John C. Breckinridge.** Breckinridge was born on 15 January 1821 near Lexington, Kentucky. After graduating from Transylvania College, he started a law practice in Lexington. He entered politics and served first as a state representative, then as a member of the US House of Representatives. In 1856, at age 35, he was elected vice president in James Buchanan's administration. Before his term as vice president ended he was elected a US senator from Kentucky. Despite Kentucky's refusal to join the Confederacy, Breckinridge accepted a brigadier general's commission in the Confederate Army. He commanded the Reserve Corps at Shiloh and was promoted to major general soon thereafter. Breckinridge fought at Vicksburg and Chickamauga. He transferred to the Eastern theater in 1864 and joined in the raid on Washington DC that year. In February 1865 he was appointed the Confederacy's last Secretary of War. After the war Breckinridge went to England and Canada. He returned to Kentucky in 1869 and resumed his law practice, dying there on 17 May 1875.

# Appendix D

## Medal of Honor Conferrals for the Battle of Shiloh

The Medal of Honor was a new award at the time of the Battle of Shiloh. President Abraham Lincoln signed into law the Medal of Honor for Navy personnel on 21 December 1861. The Army soon followed suit, and Lincoln signed the law creating the Army Medal of Honor on 12 July 1862. The Confederates did not have a medal for valor at the time of the Battle of Shiloh, so no Confederate soldiers were formally recognized for extreme bravery during the Battle of Shiloh. Four Union soldiers earned the Medal of Honor for actions during the battle.

**McDonald, John Wade.** Private, Company E, 20th Illinois Infantry. Born in Lancaster, Ohio, and entered service at Wayneville, Illinois. Citation: Was severely wounded while endeavoring, at the risk of his own life, to carry to a place of safety a wounded and helpless comrade.

**Orbansky, David.** Private, Company B, 58th Ohio Infantry. Born in Lautenburg, Prussia, and entered service at Columbus, Ohio. Citation: Gallantry in actions.

**Spalding, Edward B.** Sergeant, Company E, 52d Illinois Infantry. Born in Ogle County, Illinois, and entered service at Rockford. Citation: Although twice wounded and thereby crippled for life, he remained fighting in open ground to the close of the battle.

**Williams, Elwood N.** Private, Company A, 28th Illinois Infantry. Born in Philadelphia, Pennsylvania, and entered service at Havanna, Illinois. Citation: A box of ammunition having been abandoned between the lines, this soldier voluntarily went forward with one companion, under heavy fire from both armies, secured the box, and delivered it within the line of his regiment, his companion being mortally wounded.

# Bibliography

While not comprehensive, this bibliography provides a list of publications that are useful for staff ride preparation.

## I. Conducting a Staff Ride.

Robertson, William G. *The Staff Ride*. Washington DC: US Army Center of Military History, 1987.

This book is the US Army's "doctrine" for conducting staff rides. It offers information on organizing and conducting staff rides.

## II. Battle.

Daniel, Larry J. *Shiloh*. New York: Touchstone, 1997.

This is an excellent one-volume book on the battle. The maps are very good.

_____. *The Battle of Shiloh.* Fort Washington, PA: Eastern National Park and Monument Association, 1998.

Available from the National Park Service (on line), this is a short booklet best used when preparation time is short.

Frank, Joseph Allan and George A. Reaves. *'Seeing the Elephant': Raw Recruits at the Battle of Shiloh*. New York: Greenwood Press, 1989.

This book examines the battle from the perspective of the raw, untrained soldier. It provides interesting details on weapons and their effect on tactics.

McDonough, James L. *Shiloh—In Hell Before Night*. Knoxville: University of Tennessee Press, 1977.

This is a good one-volume book that covers the campaign and battle. The maps are not very detailed.

Sword, Wiley. *Shiloh: Bloody April*. New York: William Morrow & Co., 1974.

This is the "classic" narrative of the battle.

*The War of the Rebellion: A Compilation of the Official Records of the Union and Confederate Armies*. Vol. 10, parts 1 and 2. Washington DC: US Government Printing Office (GPO), 1886-87, 1899.

Postwar, the US government compiled and published the battle reports and correspondence from both sides. The *Official Records* (*OR*) have appeared in several reprint editions and on commercially available CD ROM. Volume 10, part 1 contains the battle reports from the commanders of both sides. Volume 10, part 2 contains the correspondence of both sides. This work is critical for serious study of the battle.

### III. Weapons and Tactics

Coggins, Jack. *Arms and Equipment of the Civil War*. Wilmington, NC: Broadfoot Publishing Co., 1987 (1962).

This very useful primer features instructive illustrations and an authoritative text. It provides a solid grounding in weapon capabilities that is essential to understanding Civil War battles.

Griffith, Paddy. *Battle in the Civil War*. Nottinghamshire, England: Fieldbooks, 1986.

This excellent booklet describes and illustrates the fundamentals of Civil War tactics in a concise, easily comprehensible format. I highly recommend it.

McWhiney, Grady and Perry D. Jamieson. *Attack and Die: Civil War Tactics and the Southern Heritage*. Tuscaloosa, AL: University of Alabama Press, 1990 (1982).

This is a controversial analysis of the Confederacy's propensity for offensive operations.

Ripley, Warren. *Artillery and Ammunition of the Civil War*. 4th Edition. Charleston, SC: Battery Press, 1984.

This comprehensive work provides technical information on artillery and ammunition.

Thomas, Dean S. *Cannons: An Introduction to Civil War Artillery*. Gettysburg, PA: Thomas Publications, 1985.

This is a very helpful primer on the technical characteristics of standard Civil War field artillery weapons.

Witham, George F. *Shiloh, Shells, and Artillery Units*. Memphis, TN: Riverside Press, 1980.

This is the comprehensive examination of artillery at Shiloh. It reviews the history, armament, and battle actions of every battery at the battle. There is also an excellent examination of artillery shells.

### IV. Combat Support and Combat Service Support

Brown, J. Willard. *The Signal Corps, U.S.A., in the War of the Rebellion*. Boston: US Veteran Signal Corps Association, 1896.

This book provides general background information such as organization, equipment, personnel, and techniques.

Freemon, Frank R. *Gangrene and Glory*. Chicago: University of Illinois Press, 2001.

This is an interesting history of medicine, both North and South, during the war.

Gillett, Mary C. *The Army Medical Department 1818-1865*. Army Historical Series. Center of Military History. Washington, DC: GPO, 1987.

This broad survey provides general background information.

Huston, James A. *The Sinews of War: Army Logistics 1775-1953*. Army Historical Series. Office of the Chief of Military History. Washington, DC: GPO, 1970.

A standard work in the field, this survey provides helpful background data on Civil War logistics.

Lord, Francis A. *They Fought for the Union*. Harrisburg, PA: Stackpole, 1960.

A wide-ranging examination of the Civil War experience, this work details organization, training, weapons, equipment, uniforms, and soldier life.

Plum, William R. *Military Telegraph During the Civil War in the United States.* Chicago: Jansen, McClurg & Co., 1882. Reprinted by Ayer Publishing Co. in June 1974.

While this may be difficult to obtain, it provides an interesting history of the telegraph during the Civil War.

## V. Biographies (Federal)

Warner, Ezra J. *Generals in Blue*. Baton Rouge, LA: Louisiana State University Press, 1964.

This standard reference work provides biographical sketches and photographs of Union general officers.

## Grant

Grant, Ulysses S. *Personal Memoirs*. 2 vols. New York: Charles L. Webster, 1885-86.

There are many good biographies of Grant, but this work is probably the best single source for a staff ride.

## Sherman

Sherman, William, T. *Memoirs of William T. Sherman*. New York: Library of America, 1990 (1885).

Again, there are many fine biographies of Sherman, but this is a good single-source work. The work cited is a revised edition published 100 years after the initial printing.

## McClernand

Kiper, Richard L. *Major General John Alexander McClernand: Politician in Uniform*. Kent, OH: Kent State University Press, 1999.

A relatively new work, this book examines McClernand as a general and explores his relationships with other generals.

## Lew Wallace

Wallace, Lew. *Lew Wallace, An Autobiography*. New York: Harper & Brothers, 1906.

Written well after the war, Wallace defends his actions at Shiloh, so read with a critical eye. This is required material for anyone researching Lew Wallace and Shiloh.

## Halleck

Ambrose, Stephen E. *Halleck: Lincoln's Chief of Staff*. Baton Rouge, LA: Louisiana State University Press, 1962.

This is a general biography that details the relationship between Halleck and Grant.

## VI.  Biographies (Confederate)

Warner, Ezra T. *Generals in Gray*. Baton Rouge, LA: Louisiana State University Press, 1959.

This standard reference work provides biographical sketches and photographs of Confederate general officers.

## Johnston

Roland, Charles P. *Albert Sidney Johnston, Soldier of Three Republics*. Austin, TX: University of Texas Press, 1964.

This is an outstanding biography of Johnston's colorful life.

## Beauregard

Williams, T. Harry. *P.G.T. Beauregard: Napoleon in Gray*. Baton Rouge, LA: Louisiana State University Press, 1955.

This is an excellent biography by a distinguished Civil War historian.

**Bragg**

McWhiney, Grady. *Braxton Bragg and Confederate Defeat*. 2 vols. New York: Columbia University Press, 1969.

Arguably, this is the best biography of Bragg by a renowned Civil War historian.

**VII.  Vignettes and First-Person Accounts**

Logsdon, David R. ed. *Eyewitnesses at the Battle of Shiloh*. Nashville, TN: Kettle Mills Press, 1994.

Available from the National Park Service, this short book is a collection of battle accounts from both sides, illuminating "the face of combat."

**VIII.  Maps**

US Department of the Interior Geological Survey. Maps can be obtained from   <http://ngmsvr.wr.usgs.gov/Other_Resources/rdb_topo.html>   or Distribution Branch, US Geological Survey, Box 25286, Federal Center Building 41, Denver, CO 80225.

1:24,000.

Pittsburg Landing TTN0541

Counce, Tennessee TTN0159

## About the Author

Lieutenant Colonel Jeffrey J. "Benny" Gudmens was born in Cincinnati, Ohio. He received a B.A. in history from the University of Dayton and an M.A. in Civil War studies from American Military University. His assignments include platoon leader and company executive officer, 82d Airborne Division; airborne company command, 6th Division; assistant G3 air, XVIII Airborne Corps during Operations DESERT SHIELD/ DESERT STORM; observer/controller, Joint Readiness Training Center; battalion operations officer, 5-20 Infantry, Fort Lewis, Washington; operations officer, Battle Command Training Program, Fort Leavenworth, Kansas; and operations adviser to the Royal Saudi Land Forces. He is currently an associate professor at the Combat Studies Institute, US Army Command and General Staff College, Fort Leavenworth.

www.ingramcontent.com/pod-product-compliance
Lightning Source LLC
Chambersburg PA
CBHW072142090426
42739CB00013B/3264